POSTCARDS FROM THE END OF THE WORLD

-

Thirty-one Years of Journeys to Israel-Palestine

by

Peter Stockton

Published in 2012 by FeedARead.com Publishing – Arts Council funded

First Edition

A CIP catalogue record for this title is available from the British Library.

Cover: Paintings by the author depicting Jerusalem in red, black, green, white and blue, the colours of the two Israeli and Palestinian flags, plus yellow bricks, a legal legacy of the British.

In the name of God, the Compassionate and the Merciful

This book is dedicated to my mother and father and my two sisters, Clare and Isobel, and to Angela.

CONTENTS

THE SITUATION – The Second Intifada & After

Introduction

This book contains nearly a hundred short pieces, stories, articles and poems (and a play) that I have written in over thirty years of visiting Israel/Palestine. This period includes the two Intifadas, literally the shaking off, the main reference points for the two parts of the book. The first Intifada ran from December 1987 until June 1993, ending with the signing of the Oslo Accords. The first part covers this period. The second part covers the period after Oslo, including the second intifada which began in September 2000 and finished in 2005.

The opening poem I wrote way back in 1981, my first ever poem, on my third day in Israel, working in the kibbutz's cotton fields. The following pieces in the first section are about the first intifada and are short, the postcards of the title in a way. They are rather sketchy and were written mainly in the Gaza Strip and on Newe Shalom/Wahat-a-Salaam, a mixed Jewish Israeli/Palestinian Israeli community, but are arranged to make a sort of narrative of a single trip, though they are taken from a number of visits. The section title, 'Someone Else's Skin', suggests something a little superficial. Maybe they are.

The second section consists of two poems. One is a diary of a week I spent in Gaza and Jerusalem on the first anniversary of the first Intifada and it really is a narrative of that week. No, it is! The second, however, although it *says* it is about a visit, was written in Oxford. What can I say? I am an artist!

The third section is a play I wrote for a BBC competition. It was shortlisted and they asked me to make some changes. They didn't like the monologue idea but they liked the location. I rewrote it but it wasn't performed. This is the monologue version again.

The fourth section is made up of four short pieces that relate to being Polish and/or Jewish, either of which I might have been had things been different. The first was inspired by the film 'Europa, Europa' and raps around the idea that Hitler was at least partly Jewish and, most significantly, circumcised. The poems are more or less autobiographical but some names have been changed. 'This Side of the Mountain' was based on a trip to Poland, though one that I survived.

In 'The Situation', the second part, there is more distance from the place than in the earlier pieces. Some of these I wrote in England and some aren't even directly about the Holy Land. 'Leaving Africa' was inspired by a part of Rian Malan's 'My Traitor's Heart', though it also echoes the ideas of origin and migration from Africa put forward by, among others, Dr Alice Roberts. She presented the idea that the first attempted leaving came up the coastal route (now Israel/Palestine) and failed. The second (successful) attempt was made, rather appositely to my line of argument, through the Arabian Peninsula. The other pieces of the fourth section were mostly written for publication in the Muslim magazine, Q-News, though 'Salaam Mr Caspie' was written as a response to an article in the Israeli paper, Ha'aretz. All were written after my conversion to Islam. They reflect this, as well they should, and they are longer. Perhaps my attention span increased as a Muslim.

They also reflect something deeper. Much as I like the 'Skin' postcards, they don't really tell people what they should think, which, freewill being well and good, is obviously what the Middle East needs. My hope is that my dual perspective may help in some way to explain how I moved from a neutral position to a committed one, at least in religious terms. As I say in some of the later pieces, as well as in another book I have written, 'Transcending Jerusalem', I believe that it is the rethinking of our religious position on the Holy Land that will, God willing, bring peace there, and hence to the world. That would be the end of the world of the title in a way, though a nod towards the more conventional big bang theory is there too, if we're not careful.

Part II of 'The Situation' consists of pieces I wrote when I was living in Nablus between 2005 and 2007. Some were published in 'This Week in Palestine'. I also wrote two of the poems in the section that follows. The third, 'An Anatomy of Longing', I wrote during a rather dry lecture in Cambridge about Iraqi Jews in Israel, while 'God is not an Elephant...' I wrote at the beginning of a sponsored bike ride from Cairo to Jerusalem. 'The Fast Show' was written in Ramadan in 2005 and is both a summary of my Holy Land experience and wishes, and an homage to the comic sketch show of the same name. 'Poem in the Sky' I wrote on the plane flying back from Israel/Palestine in 2005 and it bookends the whole in the same way that 'Poem in a Lake' bookends the other end, with a Zen-like acceptance of what is. Or something.

If you make it that far, thank you, and may God, may Allah, bless and grant peace to all who live in Israel and Palestine and to us all.

POSTCARDS FROM THE END OF THE WORLD - The First Intifada (1987-93) & Before

'We are grown-ups. We do not want to punish people who decide to visit Israel. It's not the end of the world.'

(Fadi Abboud, Lebanon's Minister of Tourism)[1]

[1] Calder, S. *How to play Middle East geo-politics,* 13th November 2010 (Independent: London)

POEM IN A LAKE

Sky-smudged cloud of charcoal grey
Forms backdrop to land's fast-enclosing night

For foreground
A dry lake
Where plumes of dust
Flow and cling and blow
On settling, sand-warmed breeze

And I
Yet smaller still
Sit
And try to catch
Or fashion
An every day
In words

I. SOMEONE ELSE'S SKIN – The First Intifada (1987-93) & Before

CONVERSATION PIECE

Tell me. What do you really think of the Palestinians?

My first, and maybe last, provocative question of the month. I am on the plane to Tel Aviv, summer, 1987, a few months before the Intifada. I am talking with David, a Jewish man who studies Applied Maths at Manchester, has lived on a kibbutz, and may come to Israel to live some day.

I cannot accept the way the Arab states have treated the refugees, he replies.

An interesting answer. He doesn't say anything more. Maybe he doesn't trust me, a *goy* who is going to work at Bir Zeit University, stronghold of Palestinian nationalism. Why should he?

My antennae, sensitised on another return to Israel, to Palestine, start twitching. From gestures, words, everyone here extrapolates, assumes, assesses. Are you with me or against me? Am I safe with you? He thinks, perhaps, not. We doze, chat a little more. He gives me his vegetarian schnitzel anyway.

He cannot accept the Arab treatment of the refugees. Humane, up to a point. He is familiar with the fact that the Palestinians have often been treated as badly, or worse, by their Arab brothers as by their Jewish cousins. For him, as far as he is prepared to go with me, the problem begins and ends there. Implicitly, the Palestinians are Arabs and have seventeen or whatever countries to choose from. There is Judea, and there is Arabia. Judea, Israel, has no responsibility for the Palestinians. She merely suffers the effects of the problem. Why do they make such a fuss over one small bit? Palestinian nationalism is a myth created by incessant propaganda, without which it would disappear. And on.

These are common beliefs, things I have heard many times, expressed with different degrees of passion, rationale, belief. Nationalism is based on qualities, feelings, that survive long after they have been exposed to logical scrutiny.

The poor man. He hardly said a thing, and already I am carrying his shadow.

CONVERSATION - PEACE

David talks across me with the old woman on my left, an Israeli from Haifa. I hear the word Hebron and ask for a translation. She supports the settlers who want to take over the market area. There was a Jewish community there until 1929 when the Palestinians killed over thirty of them and drove the rest out. Hebron is the home of the tombs of both Abraham, or Ibrahim, and his wife, and is therefore sacred to both Muslims and Jews, the burial place of the father of both faiths.

My mind begins its own trading, logically, factually, instinctively. She cries justice over Hebron. I think of the expelled Palestinians and their destroyed villages, memories only now. But I say nothing.

We get on well enough. I had given up my non-smoking seat to her allergic husband. She asked where I was going. She didn't understand my answer, Bir Zeit, the first time. She'd heard of it of course, but hadn't expected a foreigner to be going there.

You will be brainwashed, she said.

Later she talked about her daughter. She despaired that she had become religious, a fact she brought up as a comparison with me. Her own generation had been materially poor and had had to struggle. Now youth has everything and they are looking for different things. They get religion.

She used to be moody and we used to argue, she says. Now she comes home and she is helpful, she is quiet, she is polite, she says nothing. But it is terrible. She was better before!

I sit there and I listen. I have been helpful. I am quiet. Polite. I say nothing.

ARRIVAL

A Jewish woman I know bursts into tears when the plane flies over Tel Aviv. This is not because up here you can see that the planners designed the roads of the city to run parallel to the shore rather than in from it, creating the stifling breeze-free ambience of the place. No, it is a different emotion to do with coming home. Israelis call it *aliyah,* going up, when Jews come and live in Israel. A moving to a higher level of living.

The moments of arrival are pure ones, as near as that is possible. The warm air enfolds. The people are vulnerable. Children are reunited with their families, their motherland.

Hundreds await their loved ones, mostly Israelis, some Palestinians. There is little apparent tension in the night light.

A little sister is passed just over, almost into, the heads of two Palestinian girls, waiting with their mother. It is curiously unthinking. There is no apology made for invading their space. No mutual recognition. There is no, You understand. We're excited. We don't wish to be rude.

The elder Palestinian girl looks slightly uncomprehending at being unseen, completely passed over. The little girl is whisked away on a trolley by her smiling brother. Then the Palestinian brother arrives, and mother and sisters kiss and hug him, and they too are smiling.

GOLDEN DAYS

When you first see it, Israel is not like a Middle East country. It is hot, and often dusty, but this landscape in the pre-1967 Israel often frames more recent buildings, a tractor shed, a factory. Glimpses occasionally evoke Spain or France. Kibbutzim remind me of Russian collective farms, but the road to Tel Aviv and the city itself do not recall Egypt, Turkey, Syria, Jordan or Morocco. I have to wait until the West Bank and Gaza for that.

There is nothing that miraculous about much of Israel. The buildings are often already turning to seed, dilapidated, often deserted. This is another thing. There is so much emptiness, empty buildings, empty farm lands. What is all the fuss about land? And I always seem to see it from buses, surrounded by people going here, going there. I wonder where they're going, what they do for a living.

Everything looks recent, but like it's not really got going. Farms started but blew it because of the heat. Probably just my projections.

What I often wonder is, what did it all look like fifty years ago? Palestine had a population of about 800,000 then[2]. Most of them lived on the coastal plain and in the Galilee area.

I try to adopt some Golden Age Palestinian thinking, where the pre-1948 days are seen as idyllic. What grew in these fields then? How far apart were the villages? Have the old men and women who pass evocative images of the homeland on to their children seen these places now? The country must have seemed so much bigger then, without the distance-shrinking modern roads and motorways.

These are not things unique to Israel of course. But in this case the transition from pre-modern to modern is an exact point in time. Most nations experience modernisation as a process. Here it turned around the point in 1948 where Palestine became Israel, when Palestinians were expelled, and Israelis took over.

Typical Israel-Palestine stuff. Just like everywhere in the world, and completely different.

---

[2] By 2011 it was over 10 million (The Irish Times - Saturday, January 8, 2011)

ANOTHER COUNTRY

The two-state solution envisages pre-1967 Israel as the Jewish State, Israel, and the West Bank, Gaza Strip and East Jerusalem as Palestine. The doubtful simplicity of that is complicated by the existence of Palestinian towns within Israel and, most particularly, Israeli towns and settlements in the West Bank and the Gaza Strip.

It is not always obvious where you are.

I take a taxi from East Jerusalem to Gaza, crossing Israel to get there. In between the obvious Palestine and the obvious Israel are fields, rocks, dust. Neutral ground. But I see a Palestinian worker, maybe one of the few allowed out of the Strip, and I am in Palestine. I see a water filter system and wonder if it was one of the ones I assembled on the kibbutz. I assume the land is Israeli-owned. I am in Israel. And so on. It is a barely conscious thing, the mind trying to separate black from white, where a dividing line doesn't always exist.

What you see and what you get depends on what you want and what you bring. You can have a good time on a kibbutz, a holiday of 'sun, sex and slavery'. You can come and see how the Jews have made the desert bloom, brought civilisation to the Middle East. You can see how they have transformed the land and themselves after the horrors of the Holocaust and their expulsion from the Arab countries. You can meet Palestinians and hear their stories, their griefs, their horrors. See piles of rubble that were villages, houses. You can endorse every stereotype you've ever had about Jews, Israelis, Arabs, spirited, rude, intense, hospitable, bullies, victims.

Or you can ignore the present and see the religious sights, Galilee, Jerusalem, Massada, Har Megiddo, Armageddon. Many of these things, perhaps most, have associations with pain. Even those of the past are, for many, neither dim nor distant. In between all these are the same rocks, fields, trees, dust.

Most foreigners are here for a short time and that which is not their main concern will just hover on the periphery of vision. When I first came here I walked the length of the country, Mount Hermon to Eilat, with an American friend. We went through the West Bank staying in moshavim and kibbutzim. I was only dimly aware that it was a sensitive area. The maps acknowledged no distinction. As far as I was concerned, I was in Israel and I had an Israeli soundtrack in my head.

In the taxi I am surrounded by Palestinians speaking Arabic. Arab music plays. I watch out for the distinctive blue Palestinian number plates. I try to fill my head with thoughts, affirmations, that will make me comfortable here. The Israelis I see seem to be distant figures, moving in another world. But I have been there too.

WHO AM I THIS TIME?

Biblical images become muddled here. In 1981 I spent seven not very politically-aware months on a kibbutz and went to Egypt. I didn't exactly suffer under Pharaoh, but I was robbed twice and, tired of my wanderings, I abandoned my spiritual quest of getting to India and felt anxious to get back to Israel. I raced across the Sinai. My barely decent haste was met with help from Egyptians I met. One, not rich, gave me money. I did not get back in time to cross the border that day.

It was 4th June 1982 and I listened to my radio under the stars. Israel had invaded Lebanon. In my potentially dumb-assed personal mythology this border incident is my Road-To-Damascus-Conversion to an Awareness of the Palestinians' Existence. My would-be siding with the underdog was compromised by my seven months stay in Israel but rejection was not an option. Next day, as a barely conscious act of solidarity, protest, confusion and trust I hitched and walked through the Gaza Strip wearing Doc Martens, army trousers and an army T-shirt. On the advice of an Israeli I put a checked shirt over the top. I've always felt a bit like that in Gaza. Palestinians gave me lifts and dropped me off finally outside a kibbutz.

Three years later I came back to Gaza as a teacher, and after that I worked in Jericho, lowest city in the world, and the oldest, and the point at which the Jews entered Canaan under Joshua. It was also a crossing point for me, years ago, when I had whizzed through Syria and Jordan, ill and paranoid, and entered 'Israel' there, also crossing the path of my length-of-the-country walk. In Jericho I imagined myself as the garbage disposal man of the world's psyche. My face fell apart and I started writing a book.

After another eight years I came back to Gaza to teach again. Then I went down to Sinai to ask God why I thought about things, and myself, in such a ridiculous way. I got no reply, but stranded again on the same border, I saw on TV the Peace Accords of 13th September. I was beginning to wonder if this was all my fault.

People ask me, who are you? Why are you here? I want to look into their eyes and smile and say, how long have you got? But I usually say, A teacher.

ON THE BORDER

Between the poles that seem to stretch wider and wider apart - a seductive, exponential, apocalyptical image - are moments, nuances, sand shifts, looks.

At the border the soldier looks at my passport and smiles. Welcome to Gaza, he says.

Another, today, a big Ashkenazi, sergeant to three Oriental Israelis, looked me over. He asked if I spoke Arabic or Hebrew. He had a stick and a gun and a swagger, and his wink and his smile had a touch of arrogance. But it was quizzical too.

I wish I could say that in another situation we could have been friendly. Friends. That we could have talked. I imagine a bar, and him, and me, and the probable zero we would have to say to each other. In a relaxed environment, I could imagine that if we'd tried, we would be, if anything, more defensive.

Here, though, for a split second anything is possible.

For that instant we have a rapport that implicitly embraces the whole car. I almost seem to erase the words as I think them, but, yes, perhaps there can be an end to fear. We can share the land, have two equal states that trade, co-operate. Be friends even. Maybe it really could be the way the Israelis have been pretending it is for so long.

But we drive on.

I AM...

Ana mish Yahoud!

I am not Jewish.

We were taught to say this eight years ago, when a white skin in Gaza town might have meant that we were Israelis on a cheap shopping spree. Now it is more obvious that we are foreigners, *ajnabi* in Arabic, which means literally 'from the side', *etrangers* in French, with its connotations of strangeness. Only a very foolish Israeli would wander round town now, or take taxis to obscure parts of the Strip.

What may be obvious to anyone over seven is lost on the young. In a taxi, a young girl's face froze as she looked at us, in fear, though maybe in curiosity too. For her there were her own people who spoke Arabic, often darker skinned, and the Other, often pale, with their strange, incomprehensible tongue. They often wore green, and walked the streets, and they hurt her brothers, sisters, parents, neighbours.

Now she was sitting next to them in a taxi, and one of them, me, is smiling at her. The world is no longer so simple. Perhaps when she is a little older she will go into the streets and when she sees foreigners, shout 'Shalom' and throw stones at them.

When the older ones throw stones, say, outside the Islamic University, you can say it is more personal. They know you are not Israeli, but you might as well be. Your country, your culture, supports their oppression, and anyway, Jews run the White House. And Parliament. Like most here they believe what it serves them to believe.

These stones hurt more. The aim is better. The arm, stronger. The intention is greater, the act, ideological. What can you say? We are here to help you people? Robin Williams' unironic last words in 'Good Morning Vietnam'.

I am not Jewish, but the universalist vision holds true for me, of the man who said, After the Holocaust, we are all Jews.

By the same token, we are all Palestinians. We search for home, for safety, to belong, for meaning in pain, for a return to elusive childhood security, for a place where we will not fear our selves to be in danger when someone who has a different colour skin shares our taxi.

THERE BUT FOR THE GRACE OF GOD....

I have to wonder what transforms these soldiers. At times I can imagine I know how they feel, in those fleeting encounters that are something like meetings of equals, civilised beings. But perhaps I only scratch the surface. Come 9 o' clock I lose them. Off-duty I can be safe and sound at home while my alter-egos, if that's it, are kicking three types of crap out of the doors of Palestinian homes. And I could be there too, awaiting those night terrors, knowing it probably won't be tonight, but it might. It just might.

Children are famously less sophisticated, their universe far less divided. Many of those who lived through it once live in fear of the night every night, and they bed-wet and cry.

Yesterday I was at a student's house. His pretty little niece approached the room nervously and hid behind her uncle. After a while she started to smile at my copying her expressions - I threw in a few stupid ones all of my own for good measure - and she whooped with delight when I photographed her. (O, the pains of vicarious fatherhood!) But when I reached out my finger to her half-outstretched hand, she cried, and she did the same each time she thought that I was going to get nearer. After a while she started to refer to me as Al-Yahoud. Her father and uncle explained I was from England, but the distinction was lost.

She was crying when I left. For me? I wondered.

I wondered, if so, would she be asking over the next few days, in a mixture of excitement and terror, Wayn al-Yahoud? Where is the Jew?

THE GOOD SOLDIER

Are you the good soldiers?

I wonder. Two young men at a road block are asking what I'm doing, and where. They are so friendly, amused at my presence, but interested.

I say, teacher (etc).

They ask smilingly, Is it OK?

Yes, I say.

Do a good job, one of them says, just before I drive off.

A couple of weeks before, on my first day teaching, I drove towards a group of soldiers walking along the road out of a refugee camp. I didn't understand their motioning me to stop. They rapped hard on my car and ordered me out, all guns trained on me. When they realised I was English and new here they apologised. One of them said, Why do you come here? It is hell. Go back to heaven.

I almost wonder where the bastards are, the brutal ones. But people change, as do things, very quickly. Heaven to hell. Hell to heaven. Angels to villains. Villains to angels. I suspect I've met a few bastards already.

LAUGHING

A rare sight. A group of youths, *shebab*, are leaning against an army truck laughing with the soldiers.

People juggle, shuffle, emotions. One Israeli officer, an excellent Arabic speaker, works in Civil Administration. At one time students studying in the West Bank were getting an easier time when they wanted exit permits from the Strip to go back to college. (It got harder when final exams came). A line of Palestinians waits for the hoped-for permission. The officer, good at his job, maybe no stranger to torture, works down the line. Maybe he enjoys his god-like power, who knows, but he asks each one, Are you a student?

He knows, and they know he knows, and he knows they know he knows, and so on, that they're not. The laughter escalates as each one says, yes. They all get the permits.

Imagine me laughing with a soldier. In my dreams! Sure my eyes flash with something sometimes, but if I laughed, I'd be right out of here. I'm in a different game. If you're a Palestinian, laughing openly, people will understand. It is the nature of the situation.

The Palestinians in the car with me don't spit. They don't curse the laughing group. One of them says, simply, That's a rare sight.

GREY AREA

Another checkpoint, 11 at night. The soldiers are talking with a Palestinian who, you assume, has a curfew pass. They smile and wave you through. The Palestinian leaves them and asks you if he could have a lift to Jebalia camp.

You are a foreign woman and don't normally give lifts but you are driving most of the way and it's late, so you say yes. As you drive off he puts his arm across your shoulder and says you are beautiful. You are in the middle of nowhere.

Palestinian, Muslim, society has different checks and balances to those of the West. Sex is taboo outside marriage, but it happens, though not too often. One West Banker said that married women were fair game. 'The gate is already open.' Several men have rubbed their index fingers together and asked if I have a friend in England. One said, third sentence, that he liked/loved me (the word is the same in Arabic) and he clearly wanted to make something of it. As a Westerner it seems that you are often assumed to do it all the time with anybody (naked, in supermarkets, according to one.). So the questions are often asked crudely, wishing only to establish that we are different, depraved even, rather than to discover how our checks and balances work, and if indeed we have them.

We must appear quite exciting a prospect in a society that is sexually repressed when compared with our own. But such is the nature of ours that many foreigners bring some considerable confusion here and also find the 'impossibilities' curiously exciting. So it's actually no easier than at home, even if, superficially at least, it appears that that might be the case. As in this particular case.

You finally reach a junction surrounded by houses. You stop the car and tell the man to get out. He doesn't. You shout and hoot the horn. Unmoved, he tells you not to worry. You take your bag and keys and get out of the car. By now everyone is watching and you shout for help. No-one comes down, and no-one will let you phone. The man, suddenly aware of the audience, gets angry. In Hebrew and Arabic he tells everyone to go away.

The residents watch. It is after curfew. The man speaks Hebrew. They wouldn't want to side against him if the army arrive. And it's all taboo anyway. Perhaps they think you asked for it.

The drama is nearing its denouement. The two individuals and the passive audience are about to be joined by a party that changes the dynamic of the scene. Nine jeep loads of them. They too are a group who carry their own cultural confusion about power and sexuality, from a place that is quite sexually tolerant, and where wife-beating has soared since the Intifada began.

They enter and surround the car. They are kind and courteous, offer you water and are sympathetic when you cry. They arrest the man.

On the way home patrols stop you, but when they see your red face and red eyes, they are also kind. For a few moments they have all become knights in shining armour, mounted on white chargers, rescuing damsels from evil villains.

CAN YOU KEEP A SECRET?

A Palestinian child takes the good soldier a glass of tea, and she tells you this only when she trusts you, trusts you on pain of death to tell no-one.

An Israeli talks of a Palestinian family in Gaza that she and hers are good friends with. Visits aren't possible now.

It is not a war yet, though sometimes it seems so, and everyone can find justification for hatred, fear, bitterness. For all this, perhaps everyone has a moment they have shared that they hold secret in their hearts. The secret may be deeply buried, so deep that it is a secret even from the person. They are dangerous, these secrets. They are illogical, and they seem to contradict, negate, whole sets of belief systems by which people define themselves.

But we all need one, at least one, good 'Other'. If we haven't met them we will keep a place in our hearts for them, for this mythical figure to enter our lives and make us whole.

But if we have to wait too long our hearts will ache and close, and we will succumb to something like madness. In our numbness we will declare war on the other, and hence on ourselves. We will vow annihilation.

Even Eichmann learned Hebrew for two years.

FORGETTING

There was a spate of ‘collaborator’ killings in Bureij refugee camp where I was teaching, four on consecutive days at one point. Someone described a body, wide-eyed and shot through the back of the head, being dumped by masked men in the garden of the Gaza Benevolent Society.

Collaboration is a word that covers a multitude of sins, from informing to the Israelis, to cultural betrayal - drug pushers, prostitutes, thieves, members of rival political groups - or those who are involved in corruption. The collaborators may be part of family feuds. There can often be overlap, blurred edges, mixed motives.

As I drove into Bureij for my lesson I felt sensitised to this. I wondered where the killings had taken place, if any of these people had seen. I felt ashamed for them, or with them, that such things could occur. And in entertaining such thoughts, such feelings, I too felt treacherous.

Before I arrived in Gaza I dreamt a similar killing, a man and a woman stoned to death for adultery. All the people were parts of me, and I watched, horrified, seeing myself condemning and condemned, stoning and stoned.

I felt distanced from the teachers' welcoming smiles when I arrived, my thoughts stuffed with these images. My class was small. I wondered if it was because of the killings. I didn't know where it was appropriate to start or even if I could. How I could create a break from these intrusive realities with something that could allow me, us, to forget.

I seized on the first thing that came to mind and drew eleven dashes on the board, a traditional word-guessing game. Because we hadn't played this before, I elaborated. I drew a stick man, hanged. I stopped when I got to his noose, realising what I was drawing. I wondered if I should stop, but carried on and drew the gallows.

They understood the rules and guessed the word ‘interesting’, just, one leg away from, metaphorically, hanging themselves.

OCCUPATIONAL HAZARD

An incident occurs that is not untypical. A patrol is shot at. No-one is hurt. The patrol and reinforcements go to find the culprit.
They were shot at from the mosque area, but they go to a home far from the scene, too far for the 19 year-old boy they drag out to have been the gunman.

When I was stopped a few days before this, the soldier was stunned that I lived in Gaza. Maniakim! Terroristim! He gestured a throat-cutting action, implying that I should fear such a fate. I was late for a lesson, and anyway couldn't have explained that it was different for me. I'm not Israeli, I don't carry a gun. And so on.

Chicken and eggs, I thought as I drove away. For him I'm sure it would be true. There must be many in Gaza who would willingly cut his throat. Nothing personal. Occupational hazard. It would be enough that he was a soldier, and there are few families left in Gaza who haven't had someone imprisoned, beaten, wounded or killed by soldiers.

The soldiers are as impersonal. So the boy didn't do it, assuming thought gets that far, but he might have wished to. He might have done something similar before. He might do something similar in the future. (More likely, if anything, after this).

The boy protests. I am innocent. I am a student. I was studying all evening. But they put a hood over his head and beat him as they bundle him into the jeep. The hood is frightening, smelling of stale sweat, vomit, other people's terror. Suffocating. You can see nothing, and have no idea what is happening. For your captor, you the victim have become invisible, impersonal, dehumanised.

The boy's mother and other women throw stones and cry, inflaming the situation more. This, and the now pathetic wriggling of the beaten object in front of you, somehow justify these actions. You have aggravated the disease you wish to cure. In a pre-emptive way you have created the facts you wished to prove, that the Arabs are maniacs, terrorists. They all hate you. They are all the same. Animals. And should be treated as such. It is the only language they understand.

IT'S A JUMBLE OUT THERE

Under discussion is, Who will be the dominant world power in a hundred years?

Japan, China, the US still. Africa, suggests one.

No, says the Palestinian American. We have blacks back home. You can take the African out of the jungle, but you can't take the jungle...

His nephew interrupts him to disagree.

The Ethiopians here are the worst, the old one continues undaunted. Just look at them!

People agree. They are brutal.

I was stopped in Khan Younis, says the nephew. One stuck his gun up to my nose and told me to get out of the car. I said, I will. Just stand back.

His uncle wears the expression of one who has just had his point proven by an opponent, but the nephew continues.

Israel doesn't even recognise them as proper Jews. They are treated like shit. They have to prove they are better Israelis.

We understand that, he says.

But it doesn't make it any easier.

RUBBISH

We are sitting in the taxi waiting for the men to come through the checkpoint. Foreigners, women and children go straight through. One of the men gets in to rejoin his wife and two children. What went through their minds as they waited I cannot guess. The man finishes off his bottle of orangeade and throws it out of the window. It shatters.

I talk with the other woman in the taxi. She speaks excellent English and I wonder, in the annoying way I have, if I will ever see her again, and what it would be like to marry a Palestinian, her in particular, and stay here. Be in the moment, boy!

But that broken bottle bugs me. It was such an unthinking gesture. Many taxis, Palestinian, stop here, waiting for the men to come through. One, at least, will probably be delayed further by a puncture.

I really want to know, I want to ask my students, I want to ask everyone I meet, what will it be like here, if, when, the Israelis go? What I want to hear, in what is said and in what is not said, is the answer to my unasked question, who will you blame then? I will not ask this. And I will not ask, how far can you subdivide and reduce your pure, ideal community until it has no Other? When will you stop? And when all that is done, assuming there are any left, how will you begin to teach those that remain that every action, no matter how small, has consequences that will live on after you've gone. Like diamonds glistening in the sun, what shards of glass will remain in the desert sand?

A TUNNEL OF FLOWERS

Beauty should not be allowed here. It complicates things. I didn't come here to smell jasmine, or to see beautiful flowers, reds and blues, cascading over walls. I didn't come here to be kissed by beautiful children, and I certainly did not come here to be chatted up by veiled women. (She said I was handsome anyway, but would look even nicer if I cut my hair).

A lot of people agree with me. When the Intifada began, celebrations were banned. There were no parties, and weddings were sombre affairs. Punishing calls to prayer hollered out of shredded speakers five times a day. The beach was prohibited. Life has been lived in a state of continual mourning.

A stricter interpretation of Islam has spread. Faith in an authority higher than father or Fatah, the PLO, became necessary to counter the half-hearted, hopeless visions these twin pillars seemed to offer. In adopting such a strict discipline in God's name you make yourself stronger, more righteous and more right. Less prone to self-doubt, self-criticism and weakness that your enemy can exploit.

As the Palestinians have thus made themselves ungovernable, the prospect has grown that the Israelis will soon pull out. Some Palestinians fear that there will be a blood-bath when they go. People, it seems, have become a little enemy-dependant.

The stripping away of excessive, 'frivolous' activities has nonetheless raised questions about the nature of Palestinian society. Some question the wisdom of strikes that, with the Strip closed, hurt the Israelis little, and hurt the Palestinians greatly. Sometimes strikes are cancelled for this reason. Participation and enforcement reflect the nuances of commitment to the cause, a cause that can be seen as idealistic, ideological, realistic, or abject, depending at least partly on what your cause is.

I thought I would relish the polarity, see myself clearer within it, but the stripping away, like layers of onion skin, implies that a final point will be reached, that the soul will finally be bared. If that ever does happen, it hasn't happened yet.

Morning and evening I leave and enter a house that has jasmine growing over the gate. It hangs there, a beautiful, fragrant tunnel of flowers, oblivious of its environment, and to the fact that it reminds me daily what I should have realised ages ago, that life both is, and is not, that simple.

THE MAN FROM PARADISE

He sat there in the front of the taxi, a hot day, but he wore a brown anorak. A train-spotter at a party.

As the taxi pulled away he intoned the muezzin's call to prayer:

'Allah Akbar....God is the most great.'

He kept stopping, asking if it was all right, if the police would arrest him.

He was a Bosnian, a Muslim, going to Gaza, to see his sister, a nurse in Gaza or Khan Younis. Worryingly, he acknowledged no distinction.

Like a warm-up man he got the audience going. Saddam Hussein, good, he said. Arafat, bad. He will be killed. Hamas, good. Jews, Christians, we will finish.

He looked at me. His eyes were empty black holes and he asked me,

How do you feel when you see what the Serbs do to us? You have seen the TV?

I feel bad, I reply.

He asks, Bad, or very bad? There is no answer.

As the journey goes on some of the passengers become uneasy.

He asks, Are there weapons in Gaza?

No, they reply.

I was in the army for a month, he carries on, but I ran away. I can train people.

Do you have Jewish friends?

Yes, I reply.

Somewhere I think he hated me for that.

He had been staying in the Galilee, in a village called Faradees. Paradise was perhaps the only place that gave his life meaning. He is perhaps the only extremist I have met. God knows what he has seen to take him so far.

DREAM ON

I am sitting in a taxi, Jerusalem to Gaza, sleepy. On the radio, two women are talking in Arabic. I understand next to nothing.

But then, my eyes become heavy and, as I begin to doze, I come to understand exactly what they are saying.

There will be peace, and the guns will melt into the sand. They elaborate, explaining how, and it rings true. I am sure I will remember the specifics when I wake. I drift into a deeper sleep, comforted that there is peace from this conflict, within and without.

When I wake, I want to write it down, but I have no pen, the car is moving, and, as I try to hold on to what they said, it slips through my fingers like sand until I can't, for the life of me, remember anything.

KEEPING THE PEACE

Keeping the peace is at times a joke. A thoroughly pointless occupation.

An incident begins. As a UN observer it is your job to minimise the injury, and if possible to defuse the situation. This involves talking with both sides, asking soldiers to fire warning shots rather than volleys, or declaring a curfew, or asking the people to disperse.

You find an officer you can talk with, someone who will listen. Stones rain down on you both. The officer drives off and the clash escalates.

It is hopelessly one-sided. Palestinians will get killed or injured in an incident that did not 'have' to happen. But it is an honest combat, two old adversaries facing each other in the heat, bringing together years of fear, rage, humiliation, disconfirming history. They have willed it so. This clash will keep the wound open, until it heals cleanly. For a few moments the community is united. Allah wills who will die, who will be maimed or injured in the random fire.

When the fighting is over, that vision of unity and something like equality will fragment as might reasserts itself. The wounded may be arrested, there will be tension that never fully dissipates, more arbitrary killings, beatings, here or elsewhere. The situation will revert for a while to the muddled, dirty ambivalence that passes for normality.

Your task then is less foolish, but to try to stop a clash, those moments of pure adrenaline and, perhaps, truth, is like trying to suppress a moment of meaning that we as outsiders will probably never understand and certainly never wish for.

THE NEW INTIFADA

The children of the stones are today building the new state. They will drive out the idolaters, those who transgress and pollute the purity of this land.

O land of blood, we have given and will give our lives for you. O God, we pledge our hearts, our minds.

They line the streets, throngs of them. The holy ones. Men, women and children curse the soldiers, the sons of bitches who oppress them. They pick up stones, the holy stones of the land, and they hurl them.

It is curious, our role models, the patterns we repeat, the webs we trap ourselves in. We dredge history for inspiration and at times we come to the present, and find that we are repeating the grievance that has been committed upon us. We keep the wound alive, near consciousness, by replaying the role of the other. We become our own shadow.

In this, as in some other ways, these settlers, the radical Jews, have become the new Palestinians.

JEW HATER

Would you like a lift?

You are in no-man's land, at the Erez checkpoint, the entrance to the Gaza Strip. You are anxious to get out, to see some normal life, perhaps to see that Israelis aren't hateful all the time.

The accent is Brooklyn. The man is a settler. Seeing a white face he smiles. In language often, culture, religion, we foreigners are closer to the Israelis than to the Palestinians we work with. You are curious. Tempted. Who wouldn't be? A hand reaches out, so unexpected. Who would not yearn to respond?

You stand expressionless and weigh this up in an instant, knowing how the scales will always tilt. Every Palestinian and Israeli will be watching. Do you smile or are you cold? Those human radars, fine-tuned on both sides, are buzzing again, so sensitive to every nuance of that one crude question. Are you with us or against us?

What can you say? You would probably be ignored by the whole community you've been working with if you say yes. Maybe worse. The man must know this is at stake. Maybe he doesn't. The sheer chutzpah! A flicker of annoyance crosses your face.

No. I can't.

That gesture you offered, that you can offer so rarely to the world, when even your country seems about to turn on you, is thrown back in your face. It is the same as ever. Nothing has changed. You can trust no-one. No-one. The world is hateful.

You scream at the foreigner, this woman who even looks a little Jewish, but prefers the Arabs, so alien, so untrustworthy. It is the same as ever, you scream. You are a Jew hater!

As you hit the accelerator you think, in a way that is beyond thinking, of the six million, and you know why it happened, why you are here, and why you will stay.

JOURNALISIMO!

He came here full of Antipodean rage, ready to blow the gaff on the whole place.

I want the front-line, he demanded of the Palestinian Press Officer. In action he got into arguments with the Israelis.

How can you behave like this? You're treating these places like concentration camps. You Nazis!

After three such incidents the Israelis had had enough. They arrested him.

You can't do this, said the Palestinian. He's an international journalist.

We can do whatever we like, they replied.

As they led him away, he shouted, So, what are you going to do with me? Are you going to hang me up like you do the Palestinians? Bury me up to the neck in sand? Put a bag over my head? Or the hot air? Or the freezing bath?

After two hours they gave him back.

You have him, they said. And you keep him.

The next day the journalist came to the Press Officer.

Right, he said. Where's the action today?

There are no problems, the man replied. Everything is fine. There is no trouble at all.

He left.

A CURIOUS FRIEND

Sometimes you can almost forget. You can almost wonder at the tranquillity of the Strip, at the space there is, even here. Fields. People working in them. You can almost wonder if you imagined the whole thing, the pessimism, despair, hopelessness. Until you round a corner and see a line of cars at a checkpoint, suggesting strongly that you will not teach today.

But insistence can produce results, even against armed men, if you are a foreigner. You prepare yourself for assertive confrontation. What bloody-minded excuse is it this time?

They are curious, the soldiers. Arbitrary. Territorially pissing from observation posts, crapping in water cisterns, proud of their manhood and marksmanship. Two contested the latter and the winner hit a girl between the eyes.

Sometimes it is this cold, this distant. At other times it is more hot-blooded. The tension, of walking through a sea of hatred, eyes alert, trigger fingers ready, has to break sometimes. Violence ebbs and flows, waves, then calm, but always tension. Sometimes a provocation and the collective mind sees a situation where there is aggravation and the possibility of venting that tension. The possibility of expressing anger at this anonymous, hating crowd when it is small enough to be safe. The power balance you hold so precariously can be asserted, bolstered. Something breaks somewhere and you strike. As a man.

But something somewhere also hates the excesses, the daily transgressions. When settlers, men, women, some pregnant, children, attacked a Palestinian primary school after the stabbing of an Israeli girl in Israel, the soldiers were called in to escort the Palestinian children home. The day before, or maybe the day after, they could be target practice. Maybe not for this unit, but for their friends. Their countrymen.

It is Israel's Independence Day, a day that strikes a chord in the national heart. The settlers are rampaging. The soldier at the checkpoint tells you that you cannot go through. It is too dangerous. The Jews are angry today, he says.

NO CURE

In the London programme notes to 'Ghetto', a play about entertainment in the Vilna ghetto during the Second World War, its author Joshua Sobol describes his country as living "on a frozen ocean of tears." I often wonder what collective grief as done to the Israeli soul in its relations with the Palestinians and, for that matter, with each other.

In the late '70s, the band The Cure released a single, 'Killing an Arab', inspired by Camus' 'Outsider', who killed an Algerian as some existential act. They were strongly criticised for the provocative nature of the song and, as an apology, they played a benefit concert for the PLO in New York to show where their sympathies lay. During the course of this they probably also played the follow-up single, and name of the first album, 'Boys Don't Cry'.

Nearly ten years later I sat outside Jerusalem's Old City watching a march-past of teenage Israelis. They were waving the national flag and placards, egged on by a man with a megaphone. One of the boys intoned the old Cure song:

'I'm alive, I'm dead.
I am a stranger.
Killing an Arab.'

The Intifada broke out that year, and by now that same boy may have had his chance.

He may, or may not, have grown into one of the men who hated what they did, but did it anyway. One such soldier said it was worse, a hundred times worse, to be rejected as a coward by your platoon than to beat a Palestinian, but he was rejected anyway.

Some seem to enjoy the power. They beat. They shoot.

Some shoot and cry. Few just cry. Perhaps, like the boy who sang that song, the rest can't, and don't, and never could.

THE THREE PRINCESSES

Three princesses walk through the village, young girls dressed in their crowns and gowns. Two are Palestinian and one is Israeli. Their names are Peace, Light, and Hope. Salma, Nur and Tikva.

They walk in the late afternoon sun, and with every smile, every peal of laughter, every word, they bring magic to the air. A breeze stirs and carries the magic to different parts of the land.

Everywhere at that moment, people, in towns, in refugee camps, in villages, in kibbutzim, stop, if only for a second, and look around at where they are, feeling a soft stirring in their hearts. A woman doing the washing. A man in a factory. People picking fruit.

Then they carry on with whatever it is they are doing.

The three princesses walk on, talking, smiling and talking.

DOUBLE CROSSING

He is one of the *shebab*. The word means youth, though it has an edge when used by the older generation, of awe, jealousy and a little shame.

He is one of the *shebab*. Proud to be a Palestinian. Eighteen. The Intifada years were his formative years. Stone throwing. Probably detained.

He is one of the *shebab*. The nation's future on his shoulders. He has just passed exams to do a degree in Amman, Jordan, and has had his travel papers issued by the Israelis.

He goes to the Allenby Bridge and passes through the Israeli side, no problem. The two Jordanian border police look at his papers and, for no apparent reason, turn him back.

He walks back over the bridge cursing his Arab brethren. He lifts up his eyes and sees an Israeli soldier. He goes up to him and hugs him.

I love you, he says.

I love you.

I am so glad to be back.

LOOKING 4 LOVE

I decided to have an adventure and find the volunteer doctor who was working at Duyuk, a village on the outskirts of Jericho. I set off from Jericho on my bike at 8.30 to avoid the heat, so I hoped. I took the wrong road and after doubling back, was directed down a dust track. This petered out so I got off the bike and pushed it, in a constant state of pleasant expectation.

As I came into sight of a group of houses I slipped on my long trousers, in respect of local dress codes. I was eccentric. I was travelling in time. I was many things. The local barefoot acupuncturist doing his rounds. The old-style journalist digging around for dusty stories for the Times. I was Lawrence of Arabia on a bike. I imagined I looked quite dashing, and that, at any moment, a committed young doctor would emerge from a house, smiling at my flat, cloth cap and my chutzpah. I, of course, would be grinning from ear to ear.

At the houses I was received by Musa, a black Palestinian. He got his two sons to fetch coffee. I was not in Duyuk. That was a little further on. So after coffee off I went again.

In the next village I caused a stir. All work on a house stopped as the curious and the puzzled ran round me. Duyuk, I gleaned, was further on. I set off again, never once considering that I was wasting my time. No-one seemed surprised at my question, though it may have been significant that the lack of a negative doesn't necessarily indicate a positive.

I passed one more village and one more puzzled child and finally came to another main road. There was a sign pointing to Duyuk. At last I had found the place. I thought. For a moment I thought I had come to a busy medical centre, but reason soon suggested that it was a tourist spot.

Biddi shouf al-bannat angliziya, I told one of the boys in the cafe. I want to see the English woman. He led me up the path and I am sure he said that Denise was from Senegal. I had no problem with that at all.

We came to a fenced-in area that looked as little like a Medical Relief Committee building as it was possible to do. He unlocked the gate and we went in.

I'm not unappreciative of archaeology, but I was not expecting a Roman mosaic. I looked in my phrase book one last time and decided to call it a day.

HEARTLAND (A short story)

So. This is how it was, how it is, how it always will be.

The words sounded like a prayer, though she never prayed. Not now.

Yonit looked back at the man in her bed. Her boyfriend. Lover. He was asleep, as always after they made love. As often, she wasn't. She rose gently, put on her robe and went to the kitchen. She sat at the table and turned her latest sculpture round and around. The woman was large, seated with her legs pulled up, her face buried in her knees. She felt again the contours of the woman's back, the slightly rolling curves of firm flesh, smooth and warm to her touch. It would sell. She had a main occupation. This was a hobby that more than paid for itself.

She continued the massage, recalling those moments of creation, from the ball of clay, through the rough form, to the final smoothing of the skin with a moist finger. She recalled, too, the gentle kneading of her own back, less than an hour before, as they had made love.

She stopped, took her hands away, and saw the woman's beauty, her sensitivity, and her sadness.

It would sell, but she felt as she always did. Reluctant, because it was a part of herself that she wasn't ready to give up, to let go of. And making these figures somehow kept it that way.

Outside the traffic was still heavy, despite the hour. The flat, even with the windows open, was hot, thick with humidity. It wasn't a night for sleeping. This was the only time she had that she could really call her own. She put water on for coffee.

When had it started, this unease? Her life was going well. She was a busy archaeologist, a successful part-time sculptor. She had been seeing David for nearly two years, the latter part of which they'd lived together. Her parents had been hostile towards him at first. His liberal, near-atheist views, like her own, had angered the old rabbi, her father, and her mother. But they had come to accept him and welcomed him warmly now, a warmth that even extended to her. Secretly she found it hard to forgive any of them for this.

And then there was Ze'ev.

Through an irony she would never forget, even if her friends chose not to remind her, she was digging in the West Bank, excavating the ruins of an old Jewish town that had recently been discovered. So she spent her days unearthing, stone by stone, visible proof of the existence of ancient Judea, and at least some of her evenings planning ways Israel could give it back.

Ze'ev was from the nearby settlement and was responsible for the security of the dig and its diggers, a responsibility he had seemed more interested in since his first argument with Yonit.

Politics had come up early, and Ze'ev had laughed when she'd told him where she stood on the issue of the place on which they were standing.

Look. Look around you. Over there, she'd said. An Arab village. In that field. Arab workers. And there, your little settlement. Fifty houses. Half of them empty. A quarter lived in only at weekends. This is not your land! So. You surround everything with barbed wire as if it would make it yours. You still don't belong.

Look under your feet, he'd replied. A mosaic. Over there. A synagogue. I was here long before your Arabs. And I have title deeds that mean much more than some crumpled bit of paper the Turks issued. I am in every stone here. I feel it as mine, as myself. In Tel Aviv, I am a stranger. What use is Tel Aviv, what meaning is Tel Aviv, for a Jew? Nothing. Here I am a Jew. What are you?

What indeed.

So they talked like this most days, finding out about each other on the way. He was blunt. Rude even. Bearded, religious, strong, and the rest of it. And sure of himself. And unmarried. He listened to her, even if he did laugh, and he had powerful, hairy arms which she sometimes imagined enfolding her.

Perish the thought.

But there it was.

Yonit took her coffee through to the studio where she sculpted, and took a piece of clay. She began to form a figure, her fingers working quickly, purposefully, a figure of the same woman, but standing this time, facing forwards. Strong.

This was one she would keep.

SPITTING IMAGES

Coming back from West Jerusalem by bus I sit next to a man, younger than me I guess. After 20 minutes of silence we talk, and I discover he is Palestinian. I am surprised, and tell him I thought he was Israeli. No, he says. Everyone here knows the difference.

Maybe, but I think about undercover units and Palestinian Israelis.

I have seen many Palestinians who remind me of Israelis I've met. A young kibbutznik who became an Air Force pilot, and a refugee in Khan Younis. Distant cousins. Twins.

Another pair. Another Khan Younis refugee, and a student I met while hitching, from an Israeli settlement outside Nablus, Shekhem to him, on the West Bank, Samaria to him. They were both friendly, eager to talk. They looked similar, they both had scars from burns on their faces. (Maybe that's the empathy with me). And when the conversations got too deep, too dangerous, as they did pretty quickly, their similarly accented voices became shrill and we lost each other.

I don't think people do always know the difference between themselves and the Others. It's confusing. It may be reassuring at times to believe that we're all the same under the skin, but what do you do when you're the same on the surface as well? You want an image of yourself that is distinct from the Other, but you look at the Other, and it's you. A mirror image. And it's spitting at you.

EQUALS

An Israeli says, I worked with one Palestinian and I did try to treat him like an equal. He didn't know how to respond. He saw it as weak, and he tried to get away with things.

A complicated legacy.

Some day maybe it will be different, perhaps something like this?

Though the man is a soldier, though he is your occupier, he is interested in you. You are, maybe, different, perhaps the first 'Arab' he has really seen. At the roadblock, he asks you about your beliefs, the books in your bag. He is surprised that you don't believe in God.

Some day maybe you will meet again when the situation is different. He will not be in uniform, and you won't have a gun muzzle stuck in your stomach throughout the conversation.

OXYMORONS

My enemy's enemy may sometimes be my friend, but when my 'friend' is an Israeli in an undercover squad dressed as a Palestinian, the question of who my enemy is and who my friend becomes even more complicated.

Disguised groups of soldiers mingle with Palestinians, sometimes provoking situations, and sometimes hunting out wanted men. Over 150 have been killed by them since the start of the Intifada. Many of these have been shot simply for being masked - some carrying axes or chains, some just spraying graffiti. The restrictions on fire are sometimes followed. Soldiers are required to order the suspect to surrender, to warn them if they flee, and to fire at their legs if they continue to do so. But these restrictions are often ignored. There must often be a brief moment when the target realises that he is not being approached by Palestinians, but that he is about to die.

There was therefore some dark laughter when the rumour went around that an army patrol and one of these units had had a fire fight in one of the camps and that several had been wounded.

Another story had it that two patrols had been out, each unaware of the other, and had shot it out.

This was something like the story run by the Jerusalem Post, the Israeli-published English language daily. They reported a story of almost slapstick proportions of how each side had followed procedure, firing warning shots in the air, which each side had assumed was hostile. It is a story that highlights the internal contradictions of two notions dear to the life of an army, any army - military intelligence and friendly fire.

FROM A DISTANCE

From a distance I feel a lot for them. I can imagine their lives when they're at home. In the most unpromising circumstances, I still find I like them.

I was being driven in a police van to the police station, stopped for driving a terminally unroadworthy car, and talked with the policeman. He asked where I was from, why I was here.

It's a long story, I replied, quite happy to tell it. He didn't ask.

Are you frightened here?

Sometimes, I reply.

We exchanged roles. Why are you here? I ask.

It's my job. I have no choice. Unlike you.

A stone had been thrown at the van before this. He was transformed. Leapt out, breasted the closed shop windows, his gun in firing position, but not firing. My mate!

In Jerusalem I walk through the western, Jewish part of the city, Hebrew everywhere, and kippas, skullcaps. I roll my foreskin back, but it's no good. I feel very, very un-Jewish, very far from them.

It is only down here, in Gaza, that I feel that cleaving to the familiar, something more than 'there but for the grace of God go I'. In Jerusalem I feel myself to be what perhaps I am, a stranger here, far from home.

PARTY, PARTY

At 9 p.m. lives diverge. Palestinians are under curfew. The streets belong to the army. The foreigners are going to a party. Somewhere I become aware that I am not a Palestinian, and that I never will be.

I enter a little shaken. There is an army base over the road from the house, and soldiers have just told me to park my car somewhere else because it has Gaza number plates and isn't allowed there. They are, if not friendly, polite enough. Though separated by a wire fence I don't feel too far from them, playing table tennis, chatting amongst themselves. The fear I feel is not rational.

At the party I forget about the specifics of Gaza life and talk about some of my reasons for being here, psychological, intellectual stuff; I try to work out some complex emotional business with someone else; I dance; I drink. I forget, I guess, where I am.

At midnight there is noise in the street, jeeps rev up and soldiers shout. Someone says they are playing up because they've got an audience. They whoop as they drive off, and it is obvious where they are going. Their blood is up. They are not going to buy felafel.

This bravado, if that is the word, brings up a few rather disgusted comments, and I too am shocked by the relish with which they drive off for their night passage. But obscurely, intellectually, I think about the new physics, how the observer is never neutral, how they affect the interaction they are watching.

You can hear the music from the base, imagine the fun or whatever, and maybe recall similar parties of your own, in Tel Aviv. Wherever. So, what do you do? Play dominoes? Or go and kick in some doors, and the people behind them.

I felt we were implicated in the build up to that macho display and the crap-kicking that may have followed. It was sobering, and I lost my taste for dancing, for a while at least.

A TASTE FOR DANCING

In Britain, folk dancing is seen as a funny thing. Morris men and Highland flings are quaint relics of a bygone era. Here folk dancers are held in high esteem. The Dabka group we saw at Bir Zeit were famous even outside Palestine. They keep alive a culture that is in danger of being strangled. In a gesture or a rhythm they echo a history, an identity, that is held onto tenaciously because it is felt to be so fragile.

A flute introduces the village. A fluttering bird whose song echoes off the walls of the houses, a melody both oriental and Mediterranean. A drum joins that pushes a pulse, an African beat, yet delicate. Soft steps across hard-beaten, dusty earth. A voice, then a flute, then an answering chorus.

A woman introduces the dance over a solitary lute, a dance from the time when the fig and the olive were symbols of loyalty. The villagers gather round the fire and words become stories on the lips of maidens.

The dancers rise and begin. Soft shoes slide and stamp. The men, linked arm in arm, drop to their haunches like Cossacks. Then the men and women form lines and, with shouts from the audience, they beat time with claps and chants. The audience follows. The dance uses space and contrast, rises and falls. Men lead, then women. There is volume, and there is hush. The dancers drop onto one knee and the dance ends.

In the next dance, the women line up behind the men, then break into a circle. One man dips and dives around the circle like one possessed and is joined by a woman. The woman takes a tambourine and drum and offers them to the musicians as gifts of thanks. The dancers pair up and dance on.

The narrator tells that the soldiers have come and occupied the houses. The celebration is over. The family walks with only fear to feed itself. There are tears in their eyes. The smiles on their faces have disappeared.

The pipe catches a different refrain and is followed by other instruments. The dancers pace backwards. Their heads are down, but their legs are tensed and there is a spring in their step. The line breaks and the dancers join arms before returning to the individual format. Exile has begun. The dance ends.

JAFFA

Jaffa, Yafa as it was, was once a major Palestinian town and Tel Aviv a minor Jewish one. Jaffa is now a run-down enclave, surrounded, and nibbled away at, by the huge Jewish city. Houses cover the area whose groves gave the name to the oranges and the biscuits. Drugs are rife here.

A cultural pageant is being held in a monastery for the Palestinians who remain. A lute player plays music that evokes Andalucian flamenco. A band plays Arab pop and the audience forms a conga. A student from our Bir Zeit party sings nationalist songs that are well-received.

Earlier, after we'd been to the beach, some of the Palestinians from the university performed a spontaneous, musicless dabka on the beach front, receiving puzzled looks from the passing Israelis, both Jewish and Palestinian.

For the Palestinian Israelis this must have been a surprise, and possibly an alarming one. They have enough trouble being Arabs without deliberately drawing attention to the fact, and such displays are not encouraged by Jewish Israelis who prefer their Arabs quiet and anonymous. They perhaps felt the mixed feelings of the audience later that night, pride and a little shame, a feeling at once of solidarity and separation.

FOR THE LOVE OF ORANGES

Before 1948 Ashkelon was Majdal, a Palestinian town. There are still buildings from that time in what is now Migdal, a suburb of the now much larger town.

Many of the former inhabitants now live a few kilometres down the coast in the Gaza Strip. Before the Strip's closure they were able to go back and see their old lands.

Fayez' uncle visited his old orange groves, still bearing fruit. He picked an orange and died of a broken heart.

NOT THE ONLY FRUIT

What is more beautiful than the intense green of the leaves of orange trees, offsetting the splendour of the colour of their ripening fruit? An intimate balance of secondary colours reflects the softening glow of the setting sun.

Perhaps someone, somewhere, feels threatened, offended, by such manifestations of beauty, of life, for it is required that these trees, and those that bear olives, lemons, have permits. It is almost touching that these trees have an individuality, an identity, a card all of their own in some office, though such sentimentality was intended by neither the Civil Administration, nor their Creator.

Rather, it is an indirect, and very unphotogenic, form of making life difficult. You would really need two photos, one of the seductive green and orange, and another of the queue outside the Civil Administration building, maybe several, as the prospective tree planter edges nearer, perhaps over days, towards the desk that may, or may not, grant permission to grow oranges that he may, or may not, even be able to sell.

IN THE SHADOWS

It is like a childhood memory, a dimly glimpsed birth of consciousness. I was in a grapefruit orchard, picking fruit after breakfast, two days after arriving on the kibbutz, eighteen years old. Reading the Bhagavad Gita on day one, I think I'd realised I wasn't going to India.

Under the trees sat four men. They were obviously not Jewish Israelis. They offered me their food, strong, salty cheese, flat, home-cooked bread, bitter olives. I ate these strange offerings uncertainly. We had no common language so we couldn't communicate. I left after a few minutes.

I went back into the sun and carried on working. Later I found out that they owned some of the orchard, that they were Arabs.

CONSIDER THY CHILDREN...

In 1985 I visited my old kibbutz a few times while I was working in Jericho. It was a strange experience. I felt at once very at home and also very distanced, both by time and by my experience of working with Palestinians. There was much that I couldn't talk about, about what I was doing, and about how I felt, being with Palestinians and being with Israelis. Love seemed to be a word that dare not speak its name nor be understood in the context in which I felt it. I hardly understood it myself.

On Friday night in the bar I talked with a Jewish Australian woman working on the kibbutz as a volunteer from a group, the Habonim, whose aim was to bring foreign Jews to Israel to become kibbutz members. She talked about the hatred of young Israelis for the Arabs.

It's so depressing, she said, but I know that because I am a Jew, I am, and can only be, on their side. I couldn't do what you are doing without serious problems.

At breakfast next day I sat on my own and thought about the night before and about the people around me. At times, in a way that is as frightening and profound as it is ridiculous, I feel like a father visiting his children whom he's had adopted. He visits them without them knowing who he is. (Bit dishonest really). He visits them to see how they are doing.

My dear children, he says to himself, I watch you with a love you cannot know, and I cannot tell you. I watch you in your world, the world you are unable to fully understand and do not really know.

Because you are my children I can forgive you all the things you do, and I can understand and forgive your ignorance. I can do this because I love you, even if you do not know who I am.

But because I love you I feel a terror for you when I see you. I shake inside and I am washed with cold waves, because I know that the world around you that you have to ignore to protect yourselves, cares very little for you. Some day, my terror says, you, my small group of children, will have to face that very hostile world, and all the things you have done in ignorance and sometimes almost genuine innocence, will come back to you. I fear what that will do to you, and I fear what will happen then.

As I walk back from the dining room I see their children, toddling and tottering around the kibbutz, their tiny unimpressioned faces, upturned, wide-eyed and truly innocent. And my stupid love hurts.

ACTS OF LOVE

Framed against the Mediterranean is a camp. An army camp. Barbed wire surrounds it. Breeze-block guard house. Humus in tins, vegetable pate, white pita bread. Strong coffee. The slightly perfumed Time cigarettes. Blandness. Boredom. Or a harsh nicotine and caffeine hit, adrenaline rush incidents. A life stripped bare.

One guard stands in an observation post, the setting sun on his face.

I could take a stone, creep up, hurl it at him.

I walk past another military base, assess the damage I could do with a gun, a bag of grenades, from the corner that is near a sheltered street.

Or, I could ask for asylum. A protected house in the north. Tell them everything I know. His name is Ahmed. No, I don't know his family name or where he lives.

Such futile gestures, and I doubt they would achieve their objective, a breaking out of a self-imposed isolation, into the loving arms of a welcoming community, a community that perhaps defines itself as much in terms of the Other as I do.

WAITING

I met a Palestinian ex-commando. A fine-looking man. Strong, in a sinewy, muscular way, with a sharply defined, handsome face. A firm gaze. He didn't smoke and wouldn't work in Israel under any circumstances, though he is poor and needs money for education. He hates the occupation and the - as he sees them – transparently empty peace offers Israel makes.

His straightforwardness and commitment encouraged me to ask a question I do not often feel comfortable in asking.

How would you feel if Israel offered a genuine peace? One that seriously encompassed Palestinian aspirations of a return to the land and a state of their own.

He thought for a moment and said:

I would have to wait till I see it before I know.

BETWEEN A ROCK AND A HARD PLACE

Did they celebrate in Kwazulu, in Transkei, in Bophuthatswana, when the South African homelands policy was declared? Did they wave flags, dance and sing in the streets? Can you even compare?

Curiously, an Afrikaner did compare his own dream, his own predicament, the wish for a separate white state in South Africa, with the Palestinian dream of a two state solution. The world accepts theirs but not ours, he complained bitterly and, it should be said, at the time, inaccurately.

The impulse to separate is strong, impelled by fear of loss of identity, cultural erosion. Witness Hamas and the Gush Emunim, the respective outer reaches of the Palestinian and Israeli communities. If their dreams did not embrace the whole of Israel, of Palestine, they could perhaps unite against the piecemeal bantustan policies of their leaders. Strange bedfellows indeed. But they both want the same bed. And in their own religious interpretations, that is out of the question.

If you do not know who you are, if the uncrushable stone of your identity is being choked by the layers of history that have surrounded it, if you have lived so close to your projected shadow that you feel it has become a hostile, inseparable part of you, maybe it is healthy to wish to be alone. You can then discover if the stone really exists within you, if that stone really is the foundation of who you are and who you wish to become.

But shedding these layers is painful, and it is hard to let go.

Al-Awdat means 'the return' in Arabic. It can be seen as a physical thing, a return to the old homes, the old times, or it can be a metaphorical journey, a return to the self, undefined by the external 'other'.

The Gaza-Jericho autonomy agreement can be seen in these terms, a step down those perilous paths, parallel but separate. Beyond the limited vision of two bantustans can be glimpsed the shining, splendoured image of home.

But it can appear to be a trick of the light, or a dream. In the harsh light of day, the sun glares down on the minute size of this land for peace, and leaves huge unknowns in the growing shadows. Who knows what face-saving sell-outs lurk there, what compromises and secret promises. What bitterness is waiting to assert itself and declare, You do not speak for me, and I reject you.

This image feeds the nightmares of Palestinians, of the self destroying itself when left to itself. It is an image that is mirrored, for similar reasons, within Israelis.

THE DAY PEACE BROKE OUT

People line the roads, set up stalls at junctions that hand out juice, cakes, savouries. People smile and wave. Even as a foreigner I am involved. I have never seen Israelis so friendly, so generous. They ply me with food and drink. Hitching, usually so difficult, a privilege reserved for soldiers and foreign women, is easy.

I get into a car with a soldier.

What is it like up there? I ask.

It is terrible, he replies.

The uncle of a friend who works in Lebanon for the UN tells me they are dropping phosphorous bombs on Palestinians there.

It is early June, 1982. Peace has come to the Galilee.[3]

---

[3] The Israeli invasion of Lebanon in 1982 was called 'Operation Peace For The Galilee'

JOKING APART

After the Peace Accords I felt I had to leave Gaza. I couldn't bear the joy. Many people, though not everyone, wore Yasser Arafat T-shirts, or stuck posters up. With blue tack, I hoped, rather than glue. I felt at once a dread of the future, but also a feeling of having been released from an either/or way of being here.

At this time I was supposed to be renewing my visa and work permit so that I could stay longer. This involved a futile circuit of bureaucrats, and I went through the routine half-heartedly. For the Israelis, Gaza was no longer their problem.

Also, though, I felt like a traitor, for I realised that I wanted to go 'back' to Israel. Between me and everyone in those hot, familiar streets was a wall, one that I had not noticed before.

But I couldn't go 'back' to being a kibbutz volunteer, not after all this. I went, instead, to Newe Shalom, Wahat-Al-Salam, the Oasis of Peace. It is, they say, the only mixed-through-choice community in the country, a place where both Jewish and Palestinian Israelis live. I worked in the kindergarten for a week, and in the gardens for two.

One afternoon I was weeding the garden outside the guest house, helped by a Palestinian boy from Haifa who was between sessions at the Peace School. He asked, with some surprise in his voice, why I, thirty years old, was doing this, this dirty gardening work.

This was it. At last I had it, the set-up to a fabulous punch-line for a joke I'd been writing for years.

Love, I said.

We laughed.

SOMEONE ELSE'S SKIN

In the summer of 1987 after the Bir Zeit work camp we spent our last few hours in Jerusalem, wandering around the Old City and visiting the Mennonites Resource Centre, a book and video library run by Palestinians and Americans. Perhaps wondering if we'd missed something we watched videos of 'Gaza Ghetto' and 'Whose Promised Land?' Images of violence and humiliation were piled onto the stories and facts we'd heard from the people we'd met.

In 'Under A Sickle Moon' Peregrine Hodson wrote of his travels with the Mujahidin in the Afghan war. He commented that we outsiders are always protected from what we see by being outsiders. It is always someone else's story, someone else's home, someone else's life, and we always have our own that we can go back to.

I knew my way round the centre as I had been there several times before, so when we walked in we went straight to the videos, chatting and laughing, past the Palestinian woman busy at the reception desk. David and Justin are both quite dark, as was I by then. David was wearing army trousers. Those army trousers again.

We talked with the woman on the way out. She said she'd been really scared when we came in, thinking we were Israelis. She'd spent seven years in an Israeli prison.

I was shocked, and thought how temporary we were, stepping in and out of this Israeli-Palestinian problem. How must we seem, almost arrogant in our safety, walking into buildings and lives with the ease and security of the Shin Bet, Israel's internal secret police?

For a brief second I thought I could see ourselves from this woman's position.

I felt out of my depth.

IMMUNE RESPONSE

Before 1993 I had only spent a week in the country during the Intifada. I did not witness any brutality first hand but saw some of its effects on a visit to the Ahli Arab Hospital in Gaza. A man who had been walking down a street when he had been shot by an Israeli sniper. Another shot in the chest by a dumdum bullet - a normal bullet that has had its tip filed down so that it spreads on impact. The bullet had exploded in the man's chest and the pieces were still there. Another had been shot by a plastic bullet that had shattered. He had been passed over the hospital wall to avoid being arrested at the main gate.

The doctor showed us a handful of bullets that he had removed from people. Plastic, brass caps, shrapnel and aluminium. He described it as ‘experimental work with human beings’ and listed the casualties they’d treated in the first year. There had been 7,497 beatings, 730 gun- and rubber-bullet shootings, 250 tear gas inhalations, some of which had led to pregnant women miscarrying, and 20 deaths. At this point I thought, Twenty deaths? Is that all? I was shocked that I could think like this. But that was what I thought.

In Jerusalem later I met two Norwegians, a nurse and a physiotherapist, who were working in a clinic in Nablus. They said they treated victims of beatings, gassings, shootings, and of ‘chocolate bars’ that were left on the ground or thrown to children by soldiers. They exploded when they were picked up.

The physiotherapist said she was enjoying the work. She found it really satisfying and the people really good to work with. Then she actually began talking about what she was doing, getting people to walk or use limbs again after they'd been shot. Her voice changed as she spoke. It sounded hurt and almost surprised. Then the conversation became semi-technical as we discussed whether they'd been shot by dumdum bullets or not.

I find it hard to respond emotionally while I am on ‘the inside’, amidst the tension and the shock. My responses are often delayed. After my week's ‘holiday’ at the end of 1989 I came back to England and Oxford and carried on with my own life, a choice that Israelis and Palestinians do not have.

I tend to come closer to my emotions here, viewing it from the outside, and these sometimes come on suddenly. A year after my visit I was looking after an exhibition of drawings in the Oxford Library. It was entitled 'Drawn From The Fire - Children of the Intifada', a collection of 97 drawings made in Gaza and the West Bank by Canadian artist Heather Spears. In the quiet of the exhibition room I looked at the pictures and their captions.

There is a picture, of a very young girl in a shroud. Her eyes are closed, her lips slightly parted, her head is bandaged, and you can see only a little of her dark, curly hair.

'In one of the Jenin villages, while a brother and sister were playing, suddenly something exploded, injuring them dangerously and leading to the girl's death.'

There is tremendous hope in many of the pictures, 'an energy, conviction and courage', as the artist says. Many of the injured children make the victory sign, but it is in their eyes that all this can be read.

They reminded me of the eyes of the children I had met, and taught, and it was the closed eyes of the dead girl that made me cry.

DEPARTURE

I take the bus to Ben Gurion, again not looking forward to the questioning. I arrive later than I should, making the security guards suspicious. I don't like lying to them and answer their questions.

Did you meet any Arabs?

Yes.

What were their names?

I'm not prepared to tell you that. (Don’t tell them about Ahmed! Don’t tell them about Ahmed!)

She says that no harm will come to them and makes a rather perfunctory threat that I might be delayed and passed on to someone else. Hero that I am, I repeat that I won't tell them. Idiot that I am, I hope that she doesn't look in my address book.

A male security guard looks through my bags, not specially interested. Seeing my Arabic phrase book, he asks if I've learnt Arabic yet. He leafs through my 'Military Orders relating to the closure of Bir Zeit University' and my Palestinian nationalist posters and asks ironically if my battered passport has just been issued.

I wonder sometimes if it is all just volunteer paranoia or self-fulfilling prophecies that make foreigners like myself fearful of these interrogations, sending our notes and photos home by post. But the year before a woman who did tell the truth was strip-searched. It's all rather arbitrary. Another volunteer who went through at the same time as me tried to invent a story of her tour of the Holy Places and was questioned for ages. Even kibbutz volunteers miss their planes.

As I am escorted through to departures, a Palestinian son is embraced by his tearful family before he too goes up the stairs. The Israeli with me asks if I'll come back again.

I think I will, I reply.

On the way through passport control the woman there, in that Israeli way, smiles as she rudely, jokingly, questions the legibility of my exit form.

As I walk across the tarmac, I feel pulled towards tears. I walk slowly, reluctant to leave this warm air, the palm trees surrounding the airport. This place. These people.

But once up the stairs, I am in the world of air-conditioning, piped music, smiling air stewards. I could be anywhere. Except...

THE FUGITIVE

On the plane I watch the in-flight film, 'The Fugitive', an absorbing sort of film with Harrison Ford.

After the initial euphoria of the Peace Accords, the situation has been breaking down in the Territories for the last few days. Some seventy Palestinians were wounded in one day in Gaza, and today, Hamas have shot up a van outside Hebron, killing a father and son, and leaving wounded the boy's three hysterical brothers.

Watching the film, I cry for the first time in a while, partly with the film, but partly with some of the images. In a hospital scene, after a major accident, casualties in shock, screaming, crying, I see Gaza and Hebron. In the scene when the fugitive is recognised and embraced by a woman colleague, I see myself.

II. POETIC INTERLUDE

LIFE DURING WARTIME

Tender moments of reprieve
Lingering memories that tug
Today as I leave
Slender silken threads
That are stretched and spread for miles
Then snap
My stomach ties itself
Into old feelings
Loss, aloneness, unworthiness, panic
All that sort of crap
But I am doing the best I can

I become sensitised, or so I dream,
My skin up here in the ether
A sensitive membrane
Surrounded by those in prayer or smoking
In the back of the plane
Mentally unprepared
A surprise to myself
I am coming back again

Later, I'm lying on hard stone airport floors
But all is well
Peace, nor love,
Do not in an instant grow
There is a time 'twixt the time to reap
And the time to sow
That is something that anyone with the slightest knowledge of the relevant biblical passage
Should know.

War is 99% boredom
1% terror
We could walk around the City of Peace
For ever
Every stone left unthrown
Every tyre left unburned
The eve of a year of the war

And not a hair turned

A year on.
This day in Jerusalem
It is almost furtive to wander around
Looking for trouble
Chasing shadows
Soldiers walk by in threes and fours
Some outsized by tear-gas canisters
One on a horse
Another grabs the arm of a boy
At the New Gate
I stop. I wait.
He sees me.
We are ushered on.
The day passes by.
Boredom and tension
But that one per cent is gone

Entering a war zone, Gaza,
Unchallenged, unasked.
Smoke and soldiers.
Four die around us
But the next street
A different time.
We see aftermaths-
A hospital, x-rays of bullets
A beaten boy examined
On the other side of a door
Victims lie in bed
Some conscious, some not
There is nothing glorious about this
But proud? Yes.

The stories go on and on
And my thoughts go round and round
But war is displaced
By an old, old love song
And I never could sleep
In Gaza town

Cut off for another day by a strike (unofficial)
Against the two deaths yesterday (official)
Skirting round trouble
We tried to get out
And in our wanderings were questioned about
Why we are here.
I no longer fear these men in green
I don't think I ever did
Am I remaining humane
When I see myself in them
Or does it no longer touch me
The violence, the tension
The deaths and the misery?
Peace becomes an easy word
Though it is not of this world
So I have heard.

Elsewhere I have walked with impunity
Into trouble spots
And seen nothing
It stays for me
Almost unreal
Protected by an outsider's skin
Just soldiers everywhere
Pictures and stories in newspapers
Read next day
A bus fire-bombed in a place I was
An hour before.
Since I was last here in Jerusalem
There have been, it says here,
Three days of strife
A small, yet continuous,
Series of muffled explosions
The chrysalis is coming
Out of its cocoon
A time of death
Becoming
A way of life.

HARSH TREATMENT

I approach
Warily
The couch on which you lay
That is how the visit feels
This time anyway

I prepare to trawl our psyches
Illuminate our myths
We can build fragile images of momentous beauty
Eyes shining bright as we sit
Around the fire at night
Somewhere in the midst of this

You are captivated at first
I can see
(I'm sure I can)
Your eyes, they burn with hope again
We touch the idealistic man

But something in us fades
Your fingers begin to flick
Imaginary flecks of dust
That must be piling up unseen on the table in front of you
There is something in you that must kick
'That's me,'
You shrug and say
'That's all that I can do.'

Hard facts invade your consciousness
The ones that have your dreams unmade.
The thing that causes your sleeplessness
Is ready for another raid.

And when you come near this central thing –
Your fear –
You back away
Choose something else to talk about
Some minor stumbling block at which to peer

You merely want more facts to justify your truths
You do not wish to change
And so we must step outside this room
While others suffer
In the shadow of your self
As they wait for your psyche to be
Rearranged.

So
We must wait
Until next week
Until next year
During which time
We will prepare to hear
Each and every one
Except yourself
Be blamed.

III. WOZA AHMED! (A Play)

WOZA AHMAD! (A Play)

The play is set in the Gaza Strip, or South Africa, or Chechnya or Iraq, or East Timor, or Aceh... It is supposed to have a universal resonance but I imagine the actors being South African, two black, two white, or one South African who is good at accents. I only know Gaza, so the details are Israeli/Palestinian, but they could be South African, mostly.

The action occurs on one day and is revealed in four monologues, through which the story of the day, and the build-up to it, is played out.

Ahmad is an informer to the occupying authorities. Boaz is Ahmad's controller and is also briefing newly-arrived soldiers about the situation. Majid is a leader in the fight against the occupation. David is one of the new soldiers.

(Ayanqikaza Amagwala – Ladysmith Black Mambazo)
('Vukah Jonah/ Wake Up Jonah, Let Us pray' – Ladysmith Black Mambazo)

Call to Prayer

Ahmad:

You're asking, And what are you doing up at this time of day? Right? I'm praying. No, really. Five times a day. Good Muslim, that's me.

And you know what I ask God for? I pray for an end to this mess. You surprised? I do well out of it, you reckon. You don't know the half of it. I tell you. It kills me.

I work for them, yes. A while back it started. Got caught doing something, and I wasn't looking forward to a stretch in one of their jails. Wasn't sure I'd come out the other side to be honest. Politics, and treading on other people's toes, that's all I'm saying.

So this guy comes to me with an offer – big, tough guy. A couple of names of troublemakers, he says. It would help the situation, he says.

They're criminals anyway, he says. It's not collaboration, its co-operation. That's what he said.

A couple of names, they'd slap me around a bit to make it look right, send me on my way, even put a bit of cash in my pocket for the journey home. Get something for the kids, he says. Everyone does it, hahaha. Wouldn't be the first time. Do it. End of story, thank God. I thought.

Except. It never is. A couple of weeks later I got picked up again. Hadn't done anything this time, not that they've ever needed an excuse. Same guy. Obviously knows I've got problems – especially my daughter to look after. And he offers me, what can I say, regular work. And he doesn't mean in car maintenance.

And you'll be protected, he says.

What would you do? I know it's the struggle, but these people aren't exactly angels. Some of them are no better than gangs. So, I went along with it.

It was ok at first, but pretty soon you get known. Everyone starts to fear you, respect you a bit. Which made a change. They gave me a gun. Life carried on. I could live with it.

Outside anyway.

At home it was harder. My son was growing up. Understanding more. Seeing that I was getting in deeper, bit by bit. And he hated it. First of all he started complaining that the older generation were letting people down, had no guts, were corrupt. Not saying it was me, yet. Then came the looks. Suspicious. The silences. Then he was out a lot. Didn't talk at all. Not that we ever talked much. And I started to guess that he was involved. Seriously involved.

And then I got taken in one last time and the big guy says it is so. Your son is a target. He's on the list and they're going to take him out. But you can save him. Tell me where he is. I'll get him picked up. At least prison's better than losing him. No-one'll know it was you. Call me. Tell me where and when. I'll do the rest.

And then he gave me this star. A symbol of our friendship, he said. I still don't know if it was a joke.

And so they paralysed my daughter and now they're going to take my son. I'm sick of their money, and I'm sick of this mess.

Rings number on mobile

Boaz, yeah, it's me. Ahmad. You'll find him today. At the Centre. Meeting some peace delegation of yours. Finishes 11.30. Red car. Please, don't hurt him.

('Nansi Imali'/'Here is the money' – Ladysmith Black Mambazo)

Elsewhere, soldiers enter lecture room.

Boaz:

Good morning ladies, and welcome to the front line.

You may have ideas about what it's like here, you may not be looking forward to it but I want to tell you something that might make you feel a bit better about that. What you are going to face here is the real world. Everything else is dreamland. So, I mean it. Welcome.

Now, let me tell you something else. The army is something special. I would like to tell you and your mothers and fathers, that you are an important asset to us. You are precious to us. And we will upgrade you spiritually as well as physically. You will return a better person than before. This is why it is one of the most enjoyable experiences in any young man's life. But you need to know this, because you're going right in at the deep end.

Unfortunately, I cannot tell *them.* For some people, what we're doing here has become a bad word, something to be ashamed of. Don't believe it. What you will do here is something special. Let me spell this out. We are God's nation. We have civilised this place. We have civilised this place despite all the obstacles we face. The world does not understand this. The world does not understand how we've suffered, that we need to be strong, that we are fighting for our survival. The world is just going to have to accept that. I for one would rather the world hate me as I am than love me as a victim in some concentration camp. Because that is where they would like us. We are not surrounded by the Salvation Army here.

Let me tell you about them. Firstly, do not trust them. Secondly, do not trust them. If they come to you with smiles, watch yourself. Trust more the ones that show that they hate you. They hate you right to their bones, but at least it's honest. Listen, we work with some of them here. We use them, they use us. It can't last. It never lasts. Sometimes we try and get them out. Sometimes we can't. Sometimes they turn on us if they feel we've pushed them too far. But they all hate us, because they think we've made them hate themselves. At the end of the day, the only language they understand is this.

(He stamps the floor).

If we take our foot off their necks, they'll be up at our throats.

Some people would call that racism. Maybe it is. But look. I don't hate them. I think I'm better than them but I don't hate them because of that or because they're different. It's just being realistic. It's the bleeding hearts who think they can afford not to think like that but I look at them sometimes and I think, You really don't know what's going on, do you? The thing is, you're absolutely bloody right. But don't you ever wonder why there are so few of you? Most people can't think like that. People hear what goes on, but they don't believe it. They can't believe it. It would change everything if they did.

And that's where you come in. You are the elite. You carry the nation. So don't tell your girlfriends about today. Don't tell your parents. They don't want to know.

Our way of life is not perfect. We all know that. It's not ideal. We live with problems, yes. We live with things we don't like, yes. We even know that's it's wrong to think that they're dirt. But ask yourself, What is your place? Could you give it up? We don't want a mix up. You think we're gonna live together nicely if we give them some?

Why should we allow them to take what is ours? They will pollute it. They will break it.

And, it's not a bad life. It could be worse. Could be a lot worse. It's not simply power. It's comfort. Sure, some of us moan that it's others who pay, it's others who carry us but we're on top. And he's not real to us the way he is to himself. We try and feel for him we'll be shooting ourselves down.

Listen. You can't have a whole race think like that. We wouldn't last five minutes. We couldn't even get to the airport in time. And who says this anyway? All these peaceniks who went to university in the capital, a uni built on land taken from those who the bleeding hearts bleed for. They can say what they like. But even they know it's only words. It's not real. It's not real like where you live is real. It's not real like how you live is real.

We are the ones that know the score here. They can be as right as they like. No one's listening. And you, you have the right to be proud. Steel your hearts. And be proud.

Now. Today is a big day. Someone who has been giving us a lot of trouble is going to get it. All I can say is this. Get ready. Follow orders. Expect trouble.

(Inkanyezi Nezazi/The Star and the Wiseman – Ladysmith Black Mambazo)

Majid:

I understand the risks you took to get here today. But to be honest, I don't know why you came. I don't know what you have to offer and I think we have reached the point where we have to say that we can go no further. You say that you want peace, but for peace you need equality, and your people don't even come close to acknowledging that that's possible.

Your problem, the problem your people have with us, is that you do not want us here. When you see this country, you do not think of us. My country, you say. We are just an inconvenience you want to live somewhere quietly, no problems, just pop up now and then to do your filthy work. And when you can't stomach us any more, you get some scared foreigners to do it.

And all of us, you treat the same. You treat us like dirt to keep your hands clean. You try to convince yourselves that this contempt is your salvation. But you cannot escape it, because the contempt you feel is for yourselves too. So everywhere becomes conflict. Because it's in your hearts. I'd say that it shows between you and those you love, but I'm not sure the heart can love if it's that close to hate.

And what's inside is outside. Your model society looks like your heart. Your whole system is designed to poison us too. To travel out of our towns, we have to give information. To get a building permit, information. A driving licence. Information. And every time, you know it makes us hate ourselves more. Makes us trust each other less. And you know this. This is what you want. You want us to say, Without you we would be killing each other. You want us, can you believe it, to be grateful to you. I sometimes think you want us to love you for it. Because you do not love yourselves. You do not love yourselves. And we hate you for that.

Anyway, we cannot love, because of the hatred that has built in our hearts since we lost everything. Inside, everything is empty.

But what goes around comes around. And we live. We live, and we have to find a way to live with that emptiness. You, you call it terror. We, we say, It works. So what!

For you, it proves how bad we are. How much better you are. But work it out some time. How many of you have we killed? And how many of us have you killed? Sure, we kill with a knife, with a bomb. We, as you say, get our hands dirty. And maybe we dance in the streets. You, you are far away. Telescopic sights. Remote control. Guided missiles. Very clean. But at the end of the day, we are still just as dead as you.

And then there are those who survive.

I have a sister. She was walking home from school one day. I was with her. Suddenly, she trips and falls, I think. 'Cept, when she's on the ground, she can't get up. And she's lying in a pool of blood. Maybe it was some soldier showing off to his friend. Target practice. Maybe it was meant for me. I don't know. My sister is still alive, but she cannot walk now. She lies at home in bed and feels nothing.

So I have a message for you. Your peace, whatever that is and whenever, and if ever, is going to have to include her, and all those like her. And right now, you don't come remotely close. I hear you speak... listen to me... I hear your voice and I hear your words and the sound I hear is blood. Listen to me now. I look at you, even you who come to try and work with us. You who won't serve in the army. You who treat our injured. You humane ones.

And when I do, I think of our children. I think of our brothers and sisters we bury. And I know you cannot feel it like we feel it. You cannot understand how it feels to be at the mercy of someone who thinks they invented mercy. Mercy is from God. And vengeance, too, is from God.

We have tried to go down the same road together, but the time is coming when you cannot ask us to hold back, to hold on to what we have got. Because we haven't got anything. We have a new breed of children here. They believe that they are going to die. And actually they don't care.

Whatever pain we have to endure, we are prepared for it. There is a fire that is starting to burn in this land and it is burning in our hearts now. Among ourselves, we have our differences. Even we are not one family and when that day comes, we may even be killing each other to get to your homes.

But right now, right now, we see you, and we know who we are. And you cannot know how we feel to you.

When the time comes, we will have to find a new way to live in the land. But that will be our problem. Your problem will be whether you can get out in time.

That is where we are. So go. And before you come to us to talk peace, look at yourselves. But I fear it is already too late.

He leaves. An explosion is heard, followed by screams.

(Ebetlehema Yiyo Lenkosi/In Bethlehem He is King – Ladysmith Black Mambazo)

David:

I hadn't done much before I came down here. But I'd seen enough. I thought. We'd go into houses, looking for suspects, and I'd be thinking, What if this were me? Men with guns in my house? My little brother and sister?

Us guys, we were normal guys then. We'd talk, you know. We're not stupid. We'd say, We need to end this. To get out. This is killing us too. And these same guys, I watched them change. I watched me change. The first time some kid soldier beats one of them, the officer says, Man, you've finally done something properly, and you can see that the kid's sick with it, but it's also like his dad has patted him on the back and said, Well done, son. And he's proud, too. He's just passed the test. He's joined the club.

And sometimes now, you know, we enjoy it. We enjoy it. It's not just history, what we've been through as a people. We've been through school, we've been pushed around, and now people do what *we* tell them. It's cool. It's cool because without my gun, my mates, I know they'd jump me, kill me. You're on the edge there. It's a real buzz, man.

And then someone says no. And you think, What do you mean, No? Where do you get the cheek to say no from? Forget, It's wrong to be here. Forget, It's wrong to hurt anyone. What do you mean, No? I'm the law here, geddit?

I read a story. The Brits in Kenya. An officer had three of them, and one of them wouldn't stop grinning. Terrified probably, but the officer says, Stop grinning, you goon. Nothing. He hits him in the stomach. Still grinning. He hits him in the balls. Still grinning. So he puts his gun into the guy's grinning mouth and fires. Bang! Mess everywhere. The other two have done nothing. Stood like stones. So he shoots them too. What his boss says? Bury them. Clean the walls. Trying to escape. Same here.

And people wonder why we have to travel, have to get away, and then why we get hated when we go abroad. India, Thailand. Chile. You name it. It's written on our faces, man. It's in our eyes.

(Pause)

What happened today?

OK.

A big shot cell leader was hit this morning. You know that. Gunship took him out. They came onto the streets in their hundreds after that, never mind the curfew.

I was in the line with Yoni when the rocks started to come down on us. I was scared. Then Yoni got hit. Cut his head and he went down. Then this old guy runs out. Much older than the usual ones. He's got a Molotov. And he's lighting it. He lights it and he's just about to throw it and the sergeant screams at me to shoot him, and the guy looks at me as I line him up and shoot.

He falls and he's blazing and I run up to him and he's lying there screaming. He's screaming, Kill me.

I shoot him again and kick dirt over him.

He's lying there dead. And in his hand he's got a metal star.

I suddenly feel this pressure in my legs and guts.

And now I can't get it out of my head, that picture of him. His face blistering. The smell. The noise. And his voice, saying, Kill me. Kill me.

(Woza Emthonjeni/Rise Up.... – Ladysmith Black Mambazo)

(Lifikili Ivangel/Thje Gospel Has Arrived – Ladysmith Black Mambazo)

(Nkosi Sikelele Afrika – Ladysmith Black Mambazo)

IV. MY POLISH/JEWISH THING (1939 and All That)

A BIT OF SKIN

I didn't always know. I always felt different, yes. Special, yes. But I didn't know why.

At school I noticed early that other boys were different. I asked my father. He said it was what our family did. I must never ask him about it again. So he died and did not tell me. He never told me why he had shamed me so.

I first saw them when I went to Vienna. Dirty. Archaic. Strange. Foreign. It started slowly, the realisation that they were destroying everything they touched. I began to find out about them and I began to wonder.

Then my mother told me before she died that my grandfather had been a Jew, a wandering miller. She called him an old devil. Foul-mouthed. Drunk. Violent to his Christian wife and his children. Whenever I see a fawning Jew I think of him, how they would be if we gave them half a chance. He had father circumcised. Why? Was he a Jew? NO! And then father had the same done to me. He tried to make me a Jew! I am not a Jew!

I was so like my people, the German people. I was poor. A laughing stock. And yet I had dreams. I knew the majesty, the awesome power that Wagner described. And soon I began to see the cause of our misery, our failure.

One of them befriended me. Neumann. A dirty Hungarian Jew. He gave me his long, dirty, black coat. He became like my mentor. I longed to tell him my secret, but it was as if he already knew. In my mind, he was the grandfather I'd never had. The grandfather that never was. Can you imagine?

But what could I do? Neumann and his sort belonged in the gutter. If I told him my secret it would be as if we were equals. We are not the same and we never will be. I had to be rid of the likes of him, cut them out of me. I am not like him.

It was when I sensed that truth that my destiny began to unfold, and with it the destiny of the German people. It was when I recognised that the Jewish and the German soul stood for something quite opposite, and that Jewish existence cripples the true Germanic spirit, that our triumphant path opened up. With that certainty came power. All the nations that had been polluted by Jewish Marxist or liberal thinking could do nothing against the truth that I was honest enough, brave enough, to declare.

I transformed the dreams that had been sleeping for a thousand years in the German soul. I transformed those dreams through the force of my will and rode our mighty chariot against our natural enemies. I could do anything. Anything.

I felt such power, more than any man could imagine. The power of those rallies. The power I held in my hands.

Yet I could not go with a woman. I was attractive to women. They wrote to me and some would smile at me in the knowing way women have, but I could never be a man with them. To have such power and be unable to use it! Why do you think I hold my hands down here?

I am haunted by visions of thousands of dirty Jews seducing good Christian Arian women, women like my mother, and I want to put an end to their miserable, degrading race. And yes, I feel envy. I watch pornography, but it is not my destiny. I look down at myself and I know that I will seduce no-one, for if I do, everyone will know the truth, who I am, and the source of my power. I will become like the man my grandfather was, a sensual, circumcised beast, degrading the spiritual purity of my people with the only part of me that sets me apart from them; my circumcised penis.

THE OUTBREAK OF WORLD WAR II
(An Unofficial School Play)

All the conventions aspire
To make this fort assume
The furniture of home;
Lest we should see where we are,
Lost in a haunted wood,
Children afraid of the night
Who have never been happy or good.
(From, '1st September 1939' by WH Auden)

We fell into our roles
Like we were made for them
The dormitory was Europe
The beds were countries
Very simple props
The cast?

'A' was nicknamed 'Nijinsky'
After a Russian athlete,
Panto horse or ballet dancer
I could see him in a modern day 'War and Peace' as Andre
So he was Russia in this play.

'B's mother was German
So he was called 'kraut' obviously
He was small and tough
Blitzkrieg a speciality
He played a brilliant Germany.

'C' was big
'Fat White' he was called.
For me, the great White Hope:
America.
I thought he might just take my part
But did he ever?
Nope.

'D'. Guy. Guido. Yido.

Thin, ingratiating.
The weakest of us all.
This was not yet his time.
He just got it all the time.
The Jews before the Fall.

Me. Skin deep Christian arrogance
Meek and mild
Never recognised.
Victimised.
Panned.
The butt end of more jokes than anyone.
(Except for 'D').
I was, of course,
Poland.

'B' comes over to my bed one night –
Crosses the borders, so to speak,
There's nothing special about this time
He's just decided to beat me up
'Because I hate him'
He says, when asked.
He does it for real.
One take.
No need to mime.

He drags me out of bed
Throws me against the wall
As usual I don't (I can't) fight back
He winds me
Hits me in the face
It's all so fast
I fall.

No Seventh Cavalry.
'A' would perhaps have liked to do it
But it wasn't quite his style
He, and they, tried to laugh me out of it after
I lay in bed and cried the loss of God
As quietly as I could

For quite a while.

But comfort comes in many guises
I later told the year below that 'D' ****ed
(We did that sort of thing, us little elves)
I forgot it completely
He reminded me much later
We only recall the pains inflicted on our selves.

They used to take communion.
I used to ask myself how.
Now here I am writing
Semi-religious poetry
(Forgive us our sins
As we forgive those that trespass against us)
I wonder what on earth
They are doing now.

THE THIRD SON'S RETURN

My dad tells me he nearly married a Pole.
How near I came to all this Bydgoszcz stuff,
And how nearly I wasn't me at all.
So I pretend I'm coming home
To the bosom of my nearly Polish ancestry.

I have been here once and, coming back again,
Realise I'd forgotten what worked me up so before.
Brothers and father talk my head off,
One with his damnfool questions.
Through all of this I keep remembering
Being bitten on the nose
By their gun dog runt.
They're chauvinistic right to the bone and
I can't help thinking
Not a little unlike the boars they hunt.

Me, I'm a travelled son coming home for supper
I've seen a lot, been away too long,
And I see it all with different eyes.
Mother is so like one of their trappings,
At the end of the table
Or in the kitchen
Ignored
Despite her smattering of English and French.
Father talks of Soho,
'Cosmopolitan,' he says,
In the fullest sense of the word.
Or the Pigalle in Paris where,
He proudly reveals,
He went without mother.
'Maison d'amour,' she says with a look
Understanding more than we credit her for.

How much she smiles
And how little does he,
As if making up for his stolid rigidity.

And how much they smoke.
Father, in between courses, or instead,
And mother, over them as she scurries around
A gargantuan meal prepared to flatter.
Food is the way
To a man's heart they say
But all we're getting is fatter.

Father's travelled
But it hasn't broadened his mind.
He's not too soft on anyone in his beliefs,
Not on Poland or on himself.
He blames Solidarity:
'We can't travel anymore.
We had,' he opines,
'A much better life before.'
How easy life would be
If all could be explained by cause and effect.
I feel I must stop using these words,
But doubt they would notice.
They'd simply leap
Into the gaps I leave
And change the subject.

'I have changed my mind about the Jews
Since we last spoke about them'
Says the youngest
'I work with a Jewish doctor,
Typical features, big nose,'
He helpfully mimes how that looks,
'I admire them.
They are a very clever nation,'
He intriguingly calls them.

Is it that I'm lucky
To have been able to nurture
My casual humanism?
Or are they just wrong?
Their attitude to a former third of their number
I find it hard to forgive.

A gypsy woman read my palm today,
A face so like the Eastern faces that I know,
Lined but still beautiful
How many of you died
So we might live
Like this?

Father was stationed a few miles
From Treblinka in the war.
'You couldn't live with the smell
And the flames in the sky.'
It's rather late in the day
To get human about it,
But who am I
To throw stones,
To shoot and to cry.
But what is it all about?
Your pilgrimages on foot,
To worship the Black Virgin?
If it's always about two thousand years ago,
Or when you die,
What's the point of your religious fear?
It's always some other time
Some other place
But never, never now
And never here.

So, do we deserve the shit we get?
Poles have had a hard time of it
If not the hardest
(Leaving aside cause and effect and other affairs)
Butchered by the Russians in Siberia and secluded woods,
By Germans in camps and market squares
And father blames the Jews
For taking police and government posts after the war
What does he expect?
Gratitude?
'Very cruel they were.'
How little we know of ourselves.

But there is hope in youth!
One is changing his mind on the Jews.
We hope.
'Not the blacks yet?' I ask
Recalling a cinema comment three years ago.
'Perhaps you'll have changed your mind on them
By the next time I see you.'
You never know.

He goes out to get me a present.
I guess wildly and ask if it's alive
But he doesn't tell.
He brings back a hollowed-out boar's head.
'Whenever you look at it
It will remind you of your Polish friends.'
I nod sagely and see great depths
Of black humour in this
Not least a symbol of my ever-changing 'vegetable ideas'
(His charming term for my sometime vegetarianism).
Also, like me, the poor thing has suffered
The hot, growling jaws
Of their hateful little dog in its ears
The last sensation it had ever known.
They are all bloody cavemen
The lot of them.
I need,
And I'm going to need,
A lot of time on my own.

MESSAGE FROM MOUNTAIN RESCUE: Body of walker found. 10.35. 29/8

21st August.

On the journey from Krakow to the mountains of Zakopane. Place and memory brings feelings crowding back. I try to recall the bends in the road on that journey three and a half years ago. It was night then. Everything was covered in snow, cruel and gentle. The car was warm and we stopped to buy soup, me, my father, and my two Polish hosts.

At that moment I remember feeling ok, though inside I was as broken as my face looked, cracked and red with psoriasis. The intimacy of the night car journey protected me.

The situation is reversed this time. I'd been comfortably extrovert for the 36 hours of the journey until about ten minutes ago.

Yet beneath my conscious thoughts I'd been fashioning romances instinctively. This comes home to me now as I sit, alone for the first time, gazing at the gloom outside, the drizzle and occasional sunflower. My travelling friend, until now quiet and meditative, has just sat next to the first woman we'd met. Another quiet fellow traveller has moved from the seat behind to the seat next to a woman I'd talked with, deeply for a first encounter, the night before.

They're quite innocuous moves, but they convince me I'll never marry; that a brief flirtation or conversation will forever hold the power to open my heart to possibilities and then to crush it; that the pain I had stretched across Europe those years ago, down this road, to this place, that huge emptiness, is still there.

The circle is that much more vicious because a few hours before, minutes even, I had imagined that things had changed.

22nd August.

Our first full day. It is raining. I have decided to escape the weather and tour guide on a train journey north. I have started smoking again, the harsh Polish tobacco I remember from before, short stumpy little cigarettes, half Gauloise, half dust. I am nearly immune to the realisation that, half consciously, I have decided to destroy myself. The means are simply less obvious, less explicit, than those I'd considered last night.

I recall, as the train rattles on, when I have, as the phrase goes, looked destruction in the face. A typewriter, a present from my parents, whose ribbon I was trying to change. I couldn't do it. I'd felt as if my soul was being torn up like paper inside me. I looked at the typewriter, knowing there was no catharsis in its destruction. It would hurt me and my parents. I should sit down, breathe deeply, cry the pain out, talk to someone.

But I didn't. I slammed my fist down on to the keys. They buckled. I did it again. I threw the typewriter onto the floor. Then I cried. Beyond forgiveness.

Suicide I imagine (only imagine?) is like that. The despair that there is no peace on the other side. Can anyone who was ever that desperate have believed that there was enough peace or justice in the world for death to bring anything but more pain? How many have thought of family, friends, colleagues, and still said, So what. And done it.

Or those for whom the feeling is less acute, and have sought a less direct route, a risky enterprise, heavy drinking, (I light a cigarette) that small voice still saying, So what. Only quieter. Buried deeper.

Just the belief that death was a union with God, with the universe, maybe even just the suspicion that there was meaning in the world, would that not be enough to affirm life? To rouse a bit of life-saving curiosity? To pause this side? To dig in, with curses rather than prayers, with bitterness, not faith, to be tugged gently, imperceptibly, by the tide of time back into the flow.

But that is too poetic. There is nothing romantic about survival on those terms, when every day lasts forever. But it is survival.

24th August.

I stayed two nights with the hosts of last time. Some kind of habit, stupid politeness, takes me back to relive a scenario that brings out the worst in all of us; my tainted-by-victimhood siding with the underdogs, not in this case the Poles but the Jews, rubs against their ambivalent anti-Semitism. Their father talks about the stink from the gas ovens in the same breath that he talks about his spite for Jews being leading communists. They press all my buttons when I'd really rather just be able to accept them. They are far kinder to me than I'd like, or feel I deserve.

So I am torn by guilt and the question, Am I the same as them really? Is our bottom line the same?

After planning a furtive escape many times, I just told them I had to leave.

I'd talked about Auschwitz on the way over. To go or not. I've been before so should not perhaps need to go again. The questions I have cannot be answered by the enormity of Auschwitz. If I am to believe that we do create our own destinies, that they are within us, as opposed to our lives being a series of random accidents and other people's faults, then Auschwitz is infinitely terrible.

26th August.

I once imagined a journey to Poland as a quest to find some hidden part of myself, a shadow-self that, activated now, is slowly swallowing me.

Everything is a pile of shit here, and I will not do it the honour of describing it.

28th August.

Zakopane still. The coach leaves tomorrow. It has rained every day till today. Today is murky but not raining so I have left early for the mountains. I have heard of avalanches in the area. I am ill-prepared.

It is later in the day. I am miles from anywhere and the rain has started again. I am cold and I am lost. I'm not sure if I can get back.

THE SITUATION - The Second Intifada & Beyond

If
You can keep your head
When all around are losing theirs
Perhaps you've misunderstood the situation...

I. HEARTLAND - After Oslo & the Second Intifada (1993-2005)

LEAVING AFRICA (OR, A HISTORY OF THE WORLD IN 1 CHAPTER)

Many, many thousands of years ago in Africa there were many different living creatures. There was one group, though, that was different. Those in it were tall and upright, clean of limb and almost hairless. They used tools, hunted with weapons, cooked their food and buried their dead. They sensed that the life spirit was everywhere, in everything. They were the first human beings.[4]

As time passed, the numbers of this tribe grew and some of the people moved to other parts of the land, forming new tribes of their own. Later still, people began to leave Africa. Firstly, they tried to come up through the narrow strip of land that joined Africa to Eurasia, and then they crossed the sea and travelled round the edge of the Arabian peninsula.

They moved so slowly that they didn't notice that the further they went, the lighter their skins became. This was because, as the people moved north, they began to lose the sun's warmth that came to them from the skies, and the energy they drew from their connection with the source of life, the earth of Africa, so their bodies drew this energy into themselves to preserve it. As their energy left their skins, their skin became lighter and their hair straighter. Of those who came into what is now Europe, the ones who remained around the Mediterranean stayed closest to the sun. Their skin was dark and their hair black. But those who headed furthest north drew the sun further and further into themselves until their skins became quite bleached white by the mist and snow, and their hair quite straight and blond.

But it all happened so slowly that people didn't even notice.

Slowly, though, they did begin to sense that something had changed, that something was missing or that they had lost something. This made them think in a different way, in a way that they had never had to do before, because they wanted and needed to know what was lost, what was missing, what it was they had forgotten. And so in this way they became very, very clever, and the lands that they lived in reflected this.

---

[4] In Arabic, the word for human being is *insaan*, whose literal meaning is 'one who forgets'.

The lands of Egypt and Nubia produced people of genius, and the small area of land that formed the bridge between Africa and Eurasia gave birth to religions that tried, in a different way, to understand the life force, which they now called God, outside Africa. The whole area was fertile ground for the nourishment of the riches of science, art, poetry and philosophy that grew from this quest. As these gifts came further north they were honed down to their most economical, essential form, as if nothing heavier could be carried on such a long journey.

The burden that these white people had to carry, the burden that it would take them thousands of years to understand, was that they had been enlightened.

These white people were not happy, and though they tried to understand this new world, they also looked for people to blame for their unhappiness. They saw in anyone who was different to themselves, reminders of how different life had once been. So they hated and they feared people who had dark skin, because that was how they had once looked, and they feared the women amongst themselves, because they reminded them of the place of their birth and the source of their power.

However, they continued looking for answers in the world around them and as their search for knowledge took them further they began to travel the seas. Here they thought they might be able to find what it was that they sought, though they also feared that they might find monsters beyond their worst nightmares.

When they encountered the people of the other continents, they saw people who were like themselves but who were also different. Their darkness was both beautiful and frightening. To the white people they were attractive, childlike and threatening, objects of both hope and fear. The whites suspected that these people had something they, the white ones, wanted, perhaps even the very thing they were looking for.

However, though they caught glimpses of it in the treasures these people of the old lands had, and though they saw it in the eyes of the people there, they could never catch hold of it.

And though they seemed to find limitless supplies of gold and silver to rip from the earth or from the hands of the people who lived on it, and though their power gave them the power to enslave people and permitted them any licence with the women they encountered, they found neither love nor satisfaction. This made them distrust and blame the dark-skinned people even more.

But they continued searching, digging, plundering, stripping away plants and trees and soil. They continued finding new sources of power. They found coal, gas, oil, each one a transformation of the sun's energy, each one potent. The graph of progress seemed to promise to go on climbing forever.

And so, as these outer boundaries expanded, on the smallest scale the same process occurred. Brilliant men penetrated to the heart of matter, to the atom, and then, by splitting that, they were able to release more energy than had ever been imagined.

And still there was no peace.

As these people vaulted the obstacles in their way, new obstacles would appear in front of them. Old enemies would be vanquished but would appear in different form. The salvational technology became transformed into the next problem to be solved, and by this time the whole world was being affected, not just the white people.

Gradually, they began to tire. For all the energy they had tapped from the outside, they found they had little left within. It was as if they were indeed burnt out. So they began sinking where they stood, until eventually they lay prone on the ground.

After what seemed like an age, they felt a flicker in their breasts, a warm glow. This warm glow spread through their bodies, to their toes, their feet, their legs, their torsos, their backs, their fingers, their hands and their arms.

Then it spread from their breasts up their necks to their faces, until they could feel the glow behind their eyes. And when they did, they opened them.

They looked around, as if seeing the world anew, and, as their hands stretched towards each other, they looked into the eyes of their neighbours. There they saw the same light that they felt in their own hearts, and at that moment, they remembered everything.

DREAMING OF REALITY – ISRAEL AT FIFTY

And we said unto the Children of Israel after him (Moses): Dwell in the land; but when the promise of the hereafter cometh to pass We shall bring you as a crowd gathered out of various nations.
(The Qur'an 17:104)

The state of Israel was founded fifty years ago and was the crowning achievement of the Zionist movement. The Zionist idea of re-establishing the Jewish people within Palestine was as old as Jewish exile from the land, but as an effective political project its birth was during the 1890s, the decade in which Theodor Herzl published *'Der Judenstaat'* and the first Zionist conference met in Basle.

Looking at the motivations and beliefs of this movement is an experience in paradox. Zionism aimed to create a modern Jewish identity that was neither like the traditional religious nor the increasingly assimilationist one, yet it contained strong elements of both. Partly for this reason, Zionism can be all things to all people. In a book entitled 'How Israel Lost its Soul' Israeli writer Maxim Ghilan said 'It is usually from a partial ability to see things, while another part of the brain remains obscured by prejudices, that revolutionary movements arise.' It is this partial vision that dominates most views of, and in, Israel, resulting in something oxymoronic: an authoritarian democracy; an atheistic state defined and justified by religion; a Machiavellian Utopia that practices mystical *realpolitik*; a colonising liberation movement; a light unto the nations like any other. Zionists have succeeded through their ability to read the writing on the wall, though they have also written some of it themselves, and their abilities and determination have created success after short-term success that, after fifty years, have left Israelis pessimistic and with little to celebrate.

From its beginnings, though, Zionism was always pessimistic, seeing friends as enemies and vice versa. Diaspora Jews were seen as unhealthy parasites, a view often corresponding to the worst of Europe's anti-Semites, who in turn shared views about where Jews belonged ('Not here!') that could be used. The 7th Zionist Conference accused the British Prime Minister of 'open anti-Semitism against the whole Jewish people' for a 1905 speech defending the Aliens Act. In it he declared: 'A state of things could easily be imagined in which it would not be to the advantage of the civilisation of the country that there should be an immense body of persons who, however patriotic, able and industrious, however much they threw themselves into the national life, still, by their own action, remained a people apart, and not merely held a religion differing from the vast majority of their fellow countrymen, but only inter-married among themselves.' (Hansard, the House of Commons, 10th July 1905)

Twelve years later, the same Arthur Balfour wrote another declaration that was merely the other side of the coin and that gave British blessing and support to the creation of Israel.

As Europe continued to plumb the depths of anti-Semitism in the early part of the 20th century, Zionist thinking followed that of the Nazis like a shadow. When the Nazis won the 1933 election, a Zionist newspaper celebrated:

'Only rationalist newspapers who have lost the feeling for the deeper feelings of the soul, and for the origins of communal consciousness, could put aside ancestry as simply being in the realms of 'natural history'.' (*Rundschau*, 4th April 1933)

During the war, a Zionist industrialist in Switzerland, Saly Mayer, was offered the lives of all the western and Balkan Jews for $2 million by Holocaust architect Adolf Eichmann's representative, Dieter Wisleciny. Mayer refused, partly because he thought the news of mass murder was 'exaggerated tales' and partly because, as he said, 'only with blood shall we get the land.'

As late as January 1941, the Stern Gang (later to be responsible for the bombing of the King David Hotel and the massacre at Deir Yassein) sent a communiqué to the Nazis through the German Embassy in Turkey offering 'co-operation between the new Germany and a renewed volkish-national Hebrium' in the war against the Allies.

All these actions show the desperate measures that Zionists, as a minority with cosmic responsibility for the people, felt were needed. It was only after the Second World War that Zionist ideology became dominant among Jews, metaphorically and literally through a process of elimination. Before then it had been rejected by secular Jews because Zionism made it easier for anti-Semites to portray Jews as aliens and by the religious because the re-establishment of Israel was against God's will; the expulsion nearly 2000 years before had been punishment for not following the ways of God so any future restoration would be a supernatural phenomenon. The Holocaust both destroyed the dream of assimilation and asked questions of God about the Land that no one has been able to answer since. Such has been the unremitting, and partly self-created, tension since then within Israel that these deeper questions remain unfaced, frozen in an ocean of tears, as Israeli playwright Joshua Sobol puts it.

A sign of this is the secular-religious split between Israelis. Outside commentators, and many insiders, often have a post-religious mindset that inclines them to say that there would be peace were it not for the religious fanatics. The problem is essentially political. This is anathema to those with a religious way of thinking, Muslim, Christian or Jew, who find it impossible to see the return of the Jews to the Holy Land as anything other than God's will. This does not make it an issue of 'good' or even 'right', but a question of incompleteness waiting to be fulfilled within the relationship between God and his Chosen People, the Land and the Other, the descendants of Abraham from Ishmael.

The paradox in Zionism appears to be the modern development of the paradox within Judaism itself. In the Bible, the sacrifice of the 'only son' of Abraham is ambiguous. Jacob, who was later renamed Israel, meaning he who struggles with God, received his father Isaac's blessing through tricking his older brother. At the very moment of the revelation of the Ten Commandments to Moses, his brother Aaron was fashioning a golden calf for the people of Israel to pray to. (Freud, a Jew himself, understood the source of Jewish guilt to be their murder of Moses). David sent an officer to his death so that he could marry the man's wife. Their son Solomon built temples to the gods of his numerous pagan wives. In almost every defining story there is the same pattern of sage and sinner. Both are present and, echoing Maxim Ghilan above, as another Jewish writer, Dow Marmur in 'Beyond Survival', puts it: 'Whenever it (Judaism) is being presented in terms of one stream only, ignoring or denigrating its rivals, it is being falsified.'

The birth and success of Zionism has been seen as overcompensation for previous Jewish inferiority, with macho Israelis, 'drunk on the smell of steel', lording it over their new neighbours. This again has the pattern of imbalance, this difficulty in living as both wise man and warrior, which is still present in Israel today as the religious and the secular battle for the soul of Israel.

What this suggests is that this is not a holistic vision, even though it appears that at first glance there is a balance of light and dark, a way of understanding how to live with the shadow side of life.[5] On the contrary, Judaism in its Israeli context has little sense of how to deal the shadow as represented by others (whether Canaanites or Palestinians). Rather, Jewish Israelis are far more aware of the shadow in themselves as a community. 'They gazed through the Arabs with x-ray eyes' as 'psycho-historian' Jay Gonen puts it. What they see is the Land which becomes like a mirror in which they see, not God's mercy or grace, but themselves and their unhappiness because you can only be unhappy if you only consider yourself. As the Arabs have no substance, they can become projections of any historical fear. As other Jews are the only people who are 'real', the community has to carry the weight of all human love and hate. Israelis seem to hate each other for this and their brutalisation of Palestinians seems often to be incidental. Funnily enough, people are only nice to each other during wars.

In the end, Judaism's problem, and most acutely Israel's problem, is its relationship with God. As it stands, the paradox of a universal God who only has a relationship with one people is irresolvable. It calls to mind stories from the three monotheistic faiths. There are the contrasts between the stories of the would-be sacrifices of Isaac and Ishmael, of Abraham lying to Isaac in the Bible, and Ishmael submitting willingly in the Qur'an. There is the story told by Jesus in the New Testament of the prodigal son who squandered his inheritance early but was still received back by his loving and forgiving father (much to his older brother's fury). There is the story in the Bible that both Isaac and Ishmael buried their father in Hebron and were then reconciled. And there is the repeated chiding of the Jews in the Bible as 'a stiff-necked people', implying that the struggle with God will end, the heart will become a heart of flesh and the paradox of the seed of Abraham be

---

[5] One interpretation of the Israeli flag – the blue six-pointed star standing between two blue lines - is that the upwards-pointing triangle represents the land pointing to heaven, and the downward-pointing triangle triangle represents heaven pointing to earth. The two meet in Israel, between the two rivers, the Nile and the Euphrates.

resolved, if the neck softens, and body and spirit bow down in submission to the one God, Lord of All.

And you won't read that in the Oslo Accords.

POSTCARD FROM BETHLEHEM

On the northern outskirts of Bethlehem, the most famous town in the Christian world but one with a Muslim majority, lies the third holiest site in Judaism – the Tomb of Rachel, mother of Joseph (Yusuf) and Benyamin and hence, for Jews, the mother of the nation. I bought a postcard of the old building showing how it looked before it was extended a few years ago. Back then it was a small converted mosque with a nine-candle menorah on the roof that you entered through two gateposts bearing the Qur'anic inscriptions: 'And We have made every living thing of water' (21:30) and 'Their Lord will slake their thirst with a pure drink.' (76:21)

American donations have since paid for a massive extension of the building so that it is now a large modern building of clean lines and large stone blocks. Surprisingly, the two entrance posts are still in the same position relative to the velvet-covered tomb itself, though the rebuilding means that they are now inside the complex. People place lighted candles on them and, when I was there, there was a cup of tea too. A pure drink?

I was not alone there, though it was before breakfast. (Hence the tea). A Jewish man of about my age came in and prayed next to the tomb. It feels a little voyeuristic to watch but as I did I thought about our differences here in this one-time mosque-now-Jewish-shrine. It has been Judaised (almost) completely by a large building that separates the tomb physically and psychologically from the Arab town around. Armed Israeli soldiers guard it. Prayer doesn't come much safer than this. But there is no peace in Jewish prayers here. The intonation is of ritualised grief. And as he prays he rocks backwards and forwards, a ritualised formulation of the nature of being one of the Chosen People. There is the human urge to submit that takes the head into a bowing position, but almost simultaneously the will, 'the stiff neck' as extension of 'heart of stone' (the Jewish Bible credits Jews with both), brings the head back. And it goes forward. And comes back. And goes forward. And comes back. And it has gone on and on like this for centuries. These twin pulls within the heart of Judaism, animated by prayer, towards submission to, and struggle with, God.

This mother of the nation is a paradoxical figure in the Bible though. When she flees from her father Laban's house with her husband Jacob, unknown to him she steals all her father's gods, suggesting certainly a pagan upbringing and perhaps still-surviving pagan beliefs. Also, she is not the mother of the nation. She may have been Jacob's preferred wife, but it is Leah who bears Judah through whom the Children of Israel survive, and it is Leah who is buried next to Jacob in the Tomb of the Patriarchs, a few miles south from here in Hebron. Interestingly, so is Joseph, although his other tomb in Nablus is another place that is often called the third holiest place in Judaism.

In the Bible, there is a hint that the paradoxes are resolved. Isaac and Ishmael come to Hebron to bury their father. Elsewhere, there is a legend that a route to Paradise leads on from the Hebron mosque. As Muslims, we don't forget all this. As part of the five-times-daily prayers we pray the following:

'Allahumma salli 'ala Muhammad
Wa 'ala 'ali Muhammad
Kama sallayta 'ala Ibrahim
Wa 'ala 'ali Ibrahim
Wa barik 'ala Muhammad
Wa 'ala 'ali Muhammad
Kama barakta 'ala Ibrahim
Wa 'ala 'ali Ibrahim
Fil 'lamina
'Innaka hamidun majid.

Salam aleikum wa rahmat Allah

O God! Send Your grace on Muhammad and on the Family of Muhammad
As you have sent Your grace on Ibrahim and the Family of Ibrahim
And send Your blessings on Muhammad and on the Family of Muhammad
As you have blessed Ibrahim and the Family of Ibrahim
In this world and the Hereafter
For verily You are the most Praiseworthy and Glorious.

VA YOMER, VA YELEKH

Twelve Israeli actors, dressed only in black and acting in a propless white set, deliver a play, in Hebrew, that is entirely composed of passages from the Bible. Described by an Israeli journalist as 'a dialogue between 20th Century man and a holy text recited thousands of years ago', in the play the actors act, dance and sing passages that are both ancient and reflective of their own stories. It is like seeing not only the inner workings of individuals but also the whole Jewish Israeli psyche and how it relates to both God and Prophets who are at least somewhat familiar to Muslims and Christians.

The cast's biographies and often tragic family histories are given in a handout, and they resonate in the opening lines of the play from the Book of Psalms: 'My heart is in anguish within me. Fear and trembling come upon me, and I say, 'O, that I had wings like a dove! I would fly away and be at rest!'

These themes are also there in the presence of the suitcases in the play's second half. The cast are all in their twenties and thirties, yet this sense of being a mythical people carrying baggage is often intense. There is even a proud consciousness of an old graffiti slogan: The Jews are just like everyone else. Only more so.

The actors become larger than life as they enact the time when 'the history of the West took shape' (i.e. Creation); lewd in the dance of the original sin of temptation with apples and knives, linked by the play's chronology to the sins and temptations of the Promised Land; nightmarish in the desperation of Noah's flood; mocking, as three men play the voice of God declaring the law.

The story of Jeptha's daughter, who he sacrifices to God because of his military success, is repeated four times over an astonishing trance groove of increasing intensity. Biblical inconsistencies and shockers are highlighted: God's non-kosher meal with Abraham at Mamre; drunken Lot's seduction by his daughters; Joseph's father Jacob disputing his son's dream. Religion, like God, is seen as cruel and arbitrary, but both ultimately justify Israel.

The ensemble seems to hold all this in a play that has many things, but little warmth. Like Israel? I was reminded of soldiers I had seen in Gaza and at one point the black of the costumes became khaki in my mind as Joshua sent the tribes to conquer Canaan ('Va yomer, va yelekh' - 'He rose, he walked…'). They seem so supremely confident in their projections onto a sacred text that come from deep in a collective unconscious. So secure in calling God to task. And yet so unhappy, in a way that even collective history doesn't entirely explain.

My wife, herself a Palestinian, asked me what the main point of it all was when I got back. Hard to answer because, like Israel itself, this play is not a search for truth, or for a truth, or for a point, but an exploration of the mixture of myth and truth that the Bible is, an exploration that inevitably misses the point. My wife said that was what I was doing, so I had to say that the point was in the closing lines where God makes his promise to Abraham. It is, as the Israelis often say, their 'inarguable' title deed to the Land of Israel. Their point is that despite/because of all this, it is theirs: 'I will bless them that bless thee, and curse them that curseth thee: and in thee shall all families of the earth be blessed.' And: 'Unto thy seed shall I give this land.'

That Ishmael is of the seed as well as Isaac was beyond the scope of this play, as, of course, was the Muslim's five times daily blessing on the family of Abraham. It was some play certainly, but a play, or a state, that seeks to understand itself solely through the God of the Bible is, in many eyes, always going to be looking for treasure with a dodgy map.

LETTER TO THE EDITOR

To the Editor
Q News
10/3/99

In the row surrounding the Israeli Government Tourist Authority Al Aqsa poster ('In the Land where the Millennium began…the dome has already been built') people don't seem to have noticed that Israel has gone a long way in it to put an end to the controversies that have traditionally divided the monotheistic faiths. What signified the beginning of the Millennium? The birth of Jesus, the Messiah. What did the building of the Dome commemorate? The Mi'raj, the ascent into the heavens of the Prophet (salallahu aleihi wa Salaam), the event that reconnected the final (and original) religion of Islam with the faith of the Jewish Prophets (a.s.). This may not have been the plan of the poster's designers, but as it says in the Qur'an:

'And they planned, and Allah planned, and Allah is the best of planners.'

JUST SAY NO!

Arafat has given up much since Oslo so there has been a sense in the West that he let the side down at Camp David where, as Israel's Jerusalem Post put it, Israel was only one side that did the giving. How true that was we will come to, but the fact is that this time, unusually, time was on Arafat's side. Despite failing health and the ever-expanding Israeli settlements in the West Bank, it was Barak and Clinton who had the sense of urgency. For Barak this was because his government is disintegrating. For Clinton, it was because his term as President is ending and he wanted a final Middle East peace agreement to crown his term in office and fulfil his 'almost religious conviction' to make peace there. Thus, despite Arafat being the one who is usually dictated to, this time he was able to weather the storm.

Although the contents of the talks were supposed to be secret, selected details emerged, or were 'leaked', particularly regarding Israeli compromises on the status of Jerusalem. Given their nature, these can be regarded as being for both international and domestic (Israeli) consumption. Israel, it was conceded, would grant 'Joint Sovereignty' to Jerusalem, giving the Palestinians '*expanded self-administration* of *some* of the Arab Muslim quarters in the *outskirts* of Jerusalem' (my emphasis) according to Mr. Melchior, Minister for Diaspora and Social Affairs. Effectively, this was the carrot Arafat spurned, which, given its inadequacy, long-standing Middle East commentator Robert Fisk says should hardly have surprised us. (Though it still did). Where there's a carrot there's often a bigger stick, and this one, Clinton's, threatens a cut or freeze in US aid and the movement of the US embassy from Tel Aviv to Jerusalem, a move that would mean *de facto* recognition of the Holy City as Israel's capital.

On the surface of things, apart from the fact that Arafat made no major concessions (had he done so they may have cost him his life), the situation does not seem too good – some analysts have even predicted a new Intifada. However, this is something that neither side wants and there were a few positive signs that some sand shifts may yet occur in Israeli consciousness, a change the Camp David leaks may have started. As several commentators have said, to even mention a divided Jerusalem is taboo to Israelis, who grow up with the mantra of the 'eternal, united Jerusalem' in their ears. Yossi Beilin, Israel's Justice Minister says that 'these villages are not really ours… we must not allow this mirage to become an obstruction.' Though he is only referring to the villages (i.e. Abu Dis, and not the Old City or other areas of East Jerusalem like Sheikh Jarah), at least one Israeli commentator, Meron Benvenisti, has told it like it is saying, 'All this business about Israeli concessions is a sham… These 'solutions' aren't really compromises at all, simply a way of sanctifying the status quo. Much of the land that Israel claims to be 'relinquishing' wasn't Israel's in the first place.' The removal of the blot of Har Homa next to Bethlehem on Israeli 'compromise' maps is a case cited in point.

With a new US President this year, and possibly a new Israeli government too, it could go either way. The Palestinians may not even get an offer as 'good' as this one. Whatever happens, though, it is unlikely that real peace and justice can be created simply to suit the health or political timetables of any of the protagonists. There is nothing 'almost' about Jerusalem's religious significance and the timetable is ultimately in other hands.

IN A BIT OF A STATE

In the land where the Millennium began, religion sells and they now spell 'Prophet' with an 'f'. It's ophicial. Before his assassination, Rabin talked of the profit motive, and because he was speaking, he could have meant 'prophet motive'. It's a Jewish humour thing. He quipped dryly: 'No-one will come here for our winning smiles.' This throws new light on Yasser Arafat's announcement a few years back. People joked then, and wondered, did he say: 'We renounce terrorism' or, 'We *announce* terrorism'? No, no, no. It now seems that he was announcing tourism.

If this was the case, Mr Arafat must have had the New Millennium in mind, an event the people in Nazareth and Bethlehem are particularly preparing for. With the biggest birthday party in 2000 (or 2004) years imminent, O little town of Bethlehem (population 30,000) has woken to realise, for a little while at least, it will be the centre of the world. Some worry that it has woken too late – it looks like a building site. Roads are being dug up, hotels built, pipes put down.

Not to be outdone, the Israelis are preparing something called Bethlehem Israel, a charming idea involving an Arab-free Xmas experience with Jewish Israeli tour guides on land controversially confiscated in the Har Homa area and a 600m pedestrian lane from Israeli-controlled territory that will prevent tourists from seeing Palestinians at the town's checkpoint, thus confirming Ehud Barak's pledge that: 'We are here and they will be over there.' Elsewhere, there will be a virtual reality Armageddon at Har Megiddo, dubbed 'Apocalypso', and on the Sea of Galilee, an officially blessed walking-on-the-water experience.

Despite Barak's pledge, these touristic activities have made some co-operation essential. There are other profit-related activities, such as Israeli dependence on at least 100,000 Palestinian labourers from the West Bank and Gaza, and sales of Israeli goods to those areas, that make the relationship as unavoidable as it is unwished for. It is this, the demands of Realpolitik and finance rather than fraternal feelings, that have been the hallmark of the results (at best) of the Oslo Accords in 1993, and it is this that the future is being built on, in some ways literally. Ram Cohen, Industry and Trade Minister, plans to build industrial zones 'in a massive way', asking rhetorically, 'What is peace without economic agreements?'

The questions this begs are numerous, but they have to include: 'What are economic agreements without peace?' And: 'Isn't this supposed to be the Holy Land?' I'm not denying the value of a bit of cash in oiling the wheels of happiness, and after the deprivations of the Intifada, who would begrudge anyone the opportunity of living and working with some sort of security?

What is shocking is the pace at which all this is happening. The Intifada means 'the shaking off', not only of Israeli occupation but also the feelings of inferiority vis-à-vis the mighty neighbour, and even discarding some aspects of traditional Palestinian (though not Islamic) culture that were felt to be holding Palestinians down. In short, there was a revolution against a psychological imprisonment where the jailers were both within and without.

However, the results you now see suggest that the shaking off has shaken off adherence to and respect for religion and, to fill the vacuum, this has led to the embracing of the most simplistic badges of Western freedom – jeans, T-shirts, cigarettes, consumer goods – with an Arabic gloss. What typifies the ethos of this Arab pop culture is the restless, relentless vacuity of Arabic pop music and its videos, its cartoon emotions and its kitsch provocativeness. And it's everywhere – on videos, TV, in cars and taxis, shops and markets. One song (that goes 'Ay-ay-ay-oh, ay-oh-ay-oh' - you can imagine the rest) captures the zeitgeist, the spirit of the age – a subliminal wish to spend the rest of your life at your own wedding being continuously hit over the head with a silver tray as you intone the words, 'Party, party, party.' Honestly, it drives me nuts. And I haven't even mentioned the litter.

That the Israelis are ahead of this in the cultural degeneration game shouldn't be the cause of too much gloating, though. What Jewish Israelis experience, Palestinians usually get soon after – nationalism, expulsion and then religious nationalism being pertinent cases in point. As Israel seems to become more and more like California, some Jews here are becoming concerned that their children are rejecting religion. These children don't accept traditional rote learning so they either go secular or require some sort of experiential learning.

A psychological counsellor with the National Religious Youth described a pre-army religious programme as 'answering questions about God and religion better than our education system is doing.' Though not wholly applicable, there is a lesson in there for the religious everywhere.

The reason why this is happening can, some might think, be attributed to the peace process. In a book written 11 years ago, Yehoshafat Harkabi, the former head of Israeli Military Intelligence, wrote: 'If annexation is impossible and Judea and Samaria have to remain Arab, perhaps it means that the Messiah isn't after all on his way.' Even though we are only talking here about Jews actually giving up only a small percentage of the Occupied Territories, even if it were only Gaza, this is nonetheless a tremendous reverse for Israelis who combine their religion with nationalism – hence the assassination of Rabin. The 'concretising of the redemption process', as the settling of the Territories has been called, has been reversed. Though some accept this, and so seek consolation in spiritualism, others believe that nationalism, in the form of the physical ownership of all the Holy Land, is the only meaningful form of Judaism.

For Palestinians, the purity of the aims of the Intifada, that unity of purpose, is no longer there. And life is more complicated. It is harder for a Palestinian male to visit Jerusalem than it was then.

The net result is that, despite the Millennium, the Holy Land seems less holy. The religion our fathers taught us, say the young particularly, is not working. Nothing is self-evident. With the impact of post-modernism, satellite TV, Palestinian returnees and a general cultural osmosis, youth on both sides of the divide, (and of course elsewhere) find the apparent lure of 'paradise' in this life more compelling.

The challenge, as the Jewish counsellor above says, is to make the words 'live', to make learning an experience, to be modern and 'fundamentalist', to scale down the grandiose aims into something manageable, doable, liveable, to focus on the microcosm of our immediate environment without losing sight of the wider context of the macrocosm. Sheikh Hamza Yusuf speaks of how our actions within our sphere of influence (family, friends, community) feed into our circle of concern (nations), and how only concentrating on the latter does little but induce feelings of powerlessness.

It seems like another paradox, an apparent contradiction, but it suggests that we as Muslims face the implications of the Hadith where the Prophet Muhammad, on returning from battle, says: 'The lesser jihad is over. Now the greater jihad begins.' The struggle with the self.

I've decided to come and live here, so I guess that goes for me too.

HEARTS AND CORONETS

In his article about temporary marriage (*zawaj al-muta'a*)[6], Sheikh Rashid Ghannoushi says: 'Marriage in Islam is a universal law and a principal after faith for the soundness of social structures, from which human relations draw their strength, and which spreads mercy, solidarity, love, co-operation and unity.'

He also refers to the Hadith that is found at the top of the Q-Introductions page: 'By marrying, a person perfects one half of his religion... Then let him fear Allah for the other half.' This states, in practical terms, the implication of the verse: 'Your Lord created you as a single soul, and from it created its mate.' (4:1)

Both of these should guide us to the place where our true vocation as vice-regents on earth begins, and that place is the heart, and to the fact that we can only hope to achieve wholeness as human beings in marriage. Wholeness without marriage is impossible – marriage is that important.

Even in traditional Western culture this is hardly a new idea. Fairy tales have always provided children with stories that allowed profound psychological truths to be assimilated both easily and early. They spoke of princes and princesses, sometimes in disguise (as paupers), sometimes in altered form (as frogs), and sometimes unconscious (asleep for 100 years). Though it is often now considered politically incorrect, the message is that, as princesses or princes in our individual universes, we are special, and one day we will throw off our disguise, or awaken, or be transformed. This actualisation of the self will invariably be confirmed and consolidated by marriage. We will become kings and queens and live happily ever after, for which we can read, we will become whole.

Modern culture, though, goes against this and against the Qur'anic verse that says that a man's body does not contain two hearts. It almost always places seeking this 'other half' after, or instead of, marriage, as if those childhood lessons meant nothing. Film stars – modern-day princesses and princes – are literally the West's larger-than-life projections and 'the moment' is substituted for 'happily ever after.'

A debased longing for sexual fulfilment, freedom and, somehow still surviving, love, is the hybrid fruit of this culture. Though often

[6] Q-News, March 2000

shiny on the outside, it is a fruit rotten at the core, or at least, half-poisoned. And its blossom blows everywhere. It even blows here, to Palestine.

As I write, at 11.30 at night, wedding music comes from a village several miles away. It is a vivid reminder that, despite an often grim determination to bankrupt and then deafen the participants with car horns and music, marriage is an event of overwhelming importance. A coronation even. (Who can forget that 'fairytale' wedding of Charles and Diana and all the psychological baggage we had them carry down the aisle?) Yet what often happens in cultures where marriage is still prized is that the getting married, and the bald fact of being married, overwhelm the blessing of it.

The simplicity of the source of that blessing is lost in the noise and in the process of turning the bride into something a little like the wedding cake – big and white and pink. At the end of the three days – and some couples don't even make it that far – some couples must ask themselves: What was all that about? Was that me? What did it mean? And what, in the context of our lives now, does it mean?

As the basis of half our religion, the state of marital relations can be seen as a partial reflection of the state of religion, of *deen,* in East and West. A rigidity in one is likely to be reflected in a rigidity in the other. In dealing with this as the norm, we often simply react unconsciously, rather than respond consciously. This can produce sensual excesses within the faith of the kind described in an earlier issue of this magazine[7], with so-called Sufis, where the framework is ignored and a spiritual 'liberation' is sought. More often, though, it leads to the dumping of the religion altogether.

In the West this is clearly seen. Muslims simply 'integrate' themselves into the secular culture and discard both the framework and the spirit of their faith. In the East, the framework is not in question. Everyone accepts it. In theory. In practice, though, believing Muslims have often been discredited and faced with a western-orientated media onslaught that has eroded their self-confidence and left a shell-like structure of basic belief where practice is weak. Often, well-intentioned young people then justify their own weak practice on the

---

[7] Q-News, issue number 310, August 1999

basis of the emptiness, harshness and hypocrisy of the religious around them, including their parents.

All well and good – 'honest' – on the face of it, but ultimately, difficult to live with, and disastrous for the next generation. It is a gross generalisation but we don't need to look much further in the West than the current generation of black and white youth, children of parents who mostly discarded their faith, in form and belief, some time ago. Threw the baby out with the bath water, so to speak. Muslims, Hindus and other non-Western-born groups seem to be approaching this crossroads now.

So what do we do about this? It is easy to be swept along by the march of progress, the well-intentioned, morally lazy liberalisation of everything that paves this road to hell, particularly if we are wholly unconscious of it. But as the Prophet Muhammad said: 'He who knows himself, knows His Lord.' If we are to find the strength we need, we need to look in, and look at this *qalb*, this heart within.

If we go back in space, to the start of this article, and in time, to Adam, who was created vice-regent, *khalifa*, after being sent from paradise, we find the recurrent motif of the two, and hence the many, coming from the one, just as the *Tawheed*, the Oneness, of Islam gives rise to the multiplicity of Muslims. With *ibsara*, with insight, we can discern that, beneath the divinely-sanctioned separation of men and women, the protective outer and inner *hijab*, men and women are of much the same material. We are distinct, yes, but separated by the merest matter of a few genes.

Hawa (Eve) was formed of Adam's rib. This is your feminine in your masculine, and vice versa, in Chinese terms, your yin and your yang. Or your Jung: 'An inherited collective image of women exists in men's unconscious, and with the help of which he apprehends (understands) the nature of women.' That which we are unconscious of, Jung terms 'the shadow' (wherein lurk beasties). Commenting on this, Jungian writer Frieda Fordham says: 'It is when a man has repressed his feminine nature, when he under-values feminine qualities or treats women with contempt or neglect, that this dark aspect (this beastly shadow-self) is most likely to assert itself.'

We find the same language closer to home, in Sufi belief. As Martin Lings explains: 'The Divine Essence is often addressed by the Sufis as Layla, a woman's name that has the meaning of night. In this highest sense, night is the symbol of Absolute Reality in its 'feminine' aspect of Infinitude. The blue-black night sky with its stars reflects the 'womb' of Infinite Totality in which the supreme archetypes of all existing things are mysteriously contained in Oneness.'

Not entirely without justification, Muslim society is often seen as misogynistic. In order to deal with what truth there is in this and to avoid years of Jungian therapy, either collectively or individually, Muslims need look no further than the Qur'an, Hadith and the life of the Prophet Muhammad: 'And I command you to take care of women, for they are created from a rib, and the most crooked portion is its upper part. If you try to straighten it, it will remain crooked. So I command you to take care of women.' (Abu Huraira 7:114 – O.B.)

Is this not saying, Be firm and gentle with your 'other half', without and within? Choose neither force nor neglect, but the middle way of active care. And: 'Lo! Allah enjoineth justice and kindness, and giving to kinsfolk, and forbiddeth lewdness and abomination and wickedness. He exhorteth you in order that you take heed.' (16:90) This contrasts a conscious pursuit of justice and kindness to kinsfolk with the kind of promiscuous license that a culture that does not know itself is coming to regard as the norm.

In his own life, the Prophet Muhammad embraced 'feminine attributes,' just as he made no pretence of not loving his wives. As Ali reports, he even did housework! (The Shafi'i school holds that women are not obliged to do any household tasks – the marriage contract states only that the wife let her husband enjoy her sexually. The Hanafi school, however, regards housework as the wife's religious duty.)

Thirteenth Century Sufi writer and philosopher, Ibn Arabi, wrote that earthly love was like the taste of Divine love: 'If a person loves women according to the degree of the love of the Prophet, which degree is that woman is the place of effectedness and the place of the manifesting of the *haqq* (divine truth), then that man's love is Divine love, which means that he loves the *haqq* and becomes tasteful of that. Without awareness of the Divine aspect of love, it is like an image without a spirit.'

This is surely why sex outside marriage has always been a taboo in all religions – its 'image' is a diversion from the deeper aspect of love. It is also why, in a 'sexually liberated' culture, Cosmopolitan et al are constantly telling their readers that they are sexually unfulfilled.

A Hadith says that Allah gave one part of mercy to the earth and kept 99 parts with Himself. Ibn Arabi elaborates on the religious nature of love in marriage that, despite (again) its heaviness of language, touches the heart with a sense of the Divine aspect of love, as if the one part of mercy that is with humanity were reaching for its source, while the 99 parts that are with Allah, with God, come fleetingly down to us: 'When the man loved the woman through the Divine love, he demanded union. That is to say, he asked for the union which is the aim of love, and there has never been a greater union and arrival in the human genus except in the image of marriage (conjoining), like a heavy rain thoroughly penetrating the earth in the union of man and woman. In another way, one can say, in the image of the emergence of this genus there has not been a greater union than marriage, conjoining.

'The word 'marriage' is symbolical! Because of the grandeur of the union of the conjoining, at the moment of union the essential desire of the man becomes general to all parts of the person, and the desire penetrating to all parts of the man, the man finds *fana* (death, of the ego) at this point.'

Again, the image is Adamic, recalling the original conjoining of Adam and Hawa, which ultimately brought us to where we are now. In the verse: '(He) has created man from water: then he has established relationships of lineage and marriage' (25:54), we see marriage established immediately after creation. In an American talk show, the often rude (but now late) comedian, Bill Hicks, made a joke about these ancestors that, like many jokes, contained more than a seed of truth about our lack of awareness and gratitude:

'I think I learned a lot about women. I think I learned exactly how the fall of man occurred in the Garden of Eden. Adam and Eve were in the Garden of Eden and Adam said one day, 'Wow, Eve, here we are at one with nature and at one with God. We'll never age. We'll never die and all our dreams will come true the instant we have them,' and Eve said, 'Yeah. It's just not enough, is it?'

In a way it wasn't, but it was *maktoob*, written, that they should eat the fruit that drew them on and away from the path. With that act, history began and we began the long journey back to God, to Allah. But we have their lesson before us in the Qur'an, and we have within our reach if we are married, one part of a hundred of Allah's mercy.

To this, as men, we must say Al-Hamdulillah, Thank God, for a wife, who we value and cherish and grow with, is not only half of our religion but perhaps also, on this earth, the greatest reward: ‘And among His signs is this, that He created for you mates from among yourselves, that you may dwell in tranquillity with them, and He has put love and mercy between your (hearts): verily in that are Signs for those who reflect.’ (30:21)

DIARY OF AN ECLIPSE

Tuesday, 10th August 1999

The Palestinian media has been full of the eclipse for weeks. Now a national holiday has been declared – with the tone not of a holiday but of a national (natural?) emergency. There are instructions about what to do; what not to do; how to pray. Megaphone vans are driving around the parks, warning people not to even dream of going out tomorrow. Watch it on TV but don't go outside! For Israelis, though, it's a normal day.

Evening, 10th August

I didn't take it seriously at first but had an argument with a colleague who thought that the Palestinian Authority was over-reacting. It's a rare event, I said, supernatural if anything. The signs, the *ayat,* of Allah are to be read in nature, the Qur'an tells us. How much more attention shouldn't we pay if nature is of this awesome sort? This is not the time nor the place to be questioning these signs so closely. Remember the story of the wife of Saidna Lut, Lot, who was told not to look back to see the fate of Sodom but who did so and perished! Was it Shaytan who tempted her then to look on Allah's power with her own eyes at precisely the moment when she should have accepted it on trust as existing?

More than this, I said. This is a special kind of sign – it is one of the signs of the coming of the Day of Judgement, *Yawm al-Akhir*. It comes at a special time, just months before the end of the second millennium since the birth of Saidna 'Isa. And who, really, at the end of the day (or the beginning) can say that this is not the beginning of the Final Days? God knows. At the very least, though, it is a taste of that day. Prepare for your life as if you will live your life forever, and prepare for your end day as if you will die tomorrow, as a Hadith says.

Dawn, Wednesday 11th August

I woke early, and after praying I watched the sun rise. I photographed it in case it was the last time, or the at least the last time from the east! My eyes ache after. Do I imagine this? Am I going blind?

Midday, 11th August

The local TV coverage is dull. Palestinian reporters seem to be so careful that they don't even go out – just do a few shots of empty streets. When I see the coverage from other places I realise that we are rather out of sync with the rest of the world. It is probably seen as a typically Arab bit of sternness. Why always focus on the negative? Hey, just relax and enjoy it. And so on. Frankly, though, I've never known a time when Palestinians, or anyone, have been in greater need of feeling some awe for their Creator.

If our cousins and neighbours choose to be wilfully, and perhaps literally, blind to the signs, that is their look-out. As I get ready for the eclipse, I think that if the results are as bad as some say – all Palestinian doctors are on emergency alert – we might even win a war if there is one.

A man finds it overwhelming in Al-Aqsa mosque. I try to follow the prayers on TV but discover why you're not supposed to do this. After five minutes in the bowing (*ruku*) position I realise that the camera has left the mosque.

Meanwhile, Israeli TV films a reporter in the street surrounded by children. He stands on a chair and holds a piece of paper with a hole in it that projects an eclipse shadow. I try it too. It works! But I don't need a jumper outside. Or a torch. I go back inside and wait till it's over.

Thursday 12th August

The newspapers report a few cases of sight damage. My students say that the streets were quieter than during Intifada curfews, though two of them say that they spent the day driving around. Is there a hint of nostalgia here? No outbreak of mass blindness. A message to the Arab armies – Be patient.

BETWEEN DESTRUCTION AND SALVATION – from Holocaust Remembrance to Independence

With the going down of the sun on Labour Day, Holocaust Remembrance Day begins, one week before Independence Day. The existence of the former is probably little known about in Palestine, much less felt, (unlike the latter) though Palestinians know of the fact of the Holocaust. Between the extremes of Holocaust deniers and Hitler applauders, most people are aware that the forebears of their oppressors suffered enormously; that, by some mystery that has never been fully explained, Jewish suffering has been the cause of their own; and that they, the Israelis, wittingly or not, use the Holocaust to justify almost anything, with every transgression excused by the unconscious mantra, 'This is not the Holocaust.' That the Palestinian experience is 'not the Holocaust' is a given, but one thing I was reminded of again and again today is that we are invariably more aware of our own pain than that of others, whether or not we caused it.

Because of all this, my Holocaust Remembrance Day in Bir Zeit and Ramallah was felt at a slight distance, through TV, the Israeli English press and my own cultural baggage.

There were a lot of programmes, running almost continuously, mostly in Hebrew. The first in English followed US policy towards Jewish immigration in the war and showed that its harshness was responsible for many avoidable deaths, even when the facts of the Death Camps were known. The implication is that US support and aid since then has been motivated at least partly by guilt for not wanting a massive influx of Jews. Jews, the programme said, are ultimately alone. Then I went shopping.

On my way back I hailed a Service taxi going to Ramallah, 2½ shekels, and, saying I only wanted to go ½ km, gave him 1 shekel. He took it and flung it to the dashboard, muttering something hostile. He was going my way anyway and the car, though nearly empty, was leaving immediately, so from my point of view I was hardly putting the man out, and this was quite normal practice for short, in-town trips. I often wonder how much years of harsh treatment have hardened hearts to the point where rudeness is instinctive and unconscious, but I still get angry when treated like this. I hardened my heart, picked up my shekel and got out.

Back home the next programme dealt with racism and discrimination in its widest form. I came to 'Blue Eyed' half-way. A group of white Americans were sitting on the floor wearing bright green collars. On chairs around the edge sat a group that covered the range of the US's ethnic minorities, African, Asian, men, women, old, young. A white-haired, blue-eyed woman, Jane Elliot, was running the workshop, 'teaching' the green collar group, getting them to write down the rules of good listening as she dictated them. And she, fully in role as 'oppressor', was giving them hell. They could do nothing right and she was bitingly personal in her comments on these 'pupils'. One she ridiculed for her Valley Girl persona. 'Get over cute. Get qualified or by the time you're 45 you'll be passed over for any promotion.' Another – 'When you look up at me get that grin off your face.' And another man who wanted to know that she 'cared' she brought to tears.

As these scenes were intercut with interviews with her and previous participants, a fuller picture emerged of where she was coming from. As she drove through her neighbourhood in the autumn she said, 'The trees here are really beautiful. All colours. This is a community that is proud of that. But they won't let people of colour live here.' And, quoting President Reagan, asked on camera as he inaugurated Martin Luther King Day whether King was a communist, who said, 'Well, we'll find out in 30 years, won't we?' The message? We'll give them this day but let's be clear about how we feel about it and about who has the power. And clips from 25 years ago when kids from her school did the same experiment – clearly stated, 'Blue eyed kids are better, brown eyed kids are stupid.' A Jewish woman said to her then, despite the careful controls and the profound insights the kids got, 'I hate you. You created in that class the atmosphere of Nazi Germany in the 30s.'

Towards the end she asked those sitting around the white group if they wanted to volunteer anything, any comments on the suffering and anguish the whites had endured for 2½ hours. And everyone who spoke said the same. Black. Asian. Old. Young. Disabled. Men. Women. This is what we live. Every day. This is what we send our children out into. This gut sickness they feel now we live with. Knowing it's wrong is no help. There is no protection from it. And it kills.

The programme was in English with Hebrew and Arabic subtitles. It may not have been intended to do so but the programme thus resonated with every level of oppression here, historical and present,

Goyim and Jews, white Jews and black, or brown, Israelis and Palestinians, men and women. And is it taxi drivers and foreigners? Or foreigners and taxi drivers? I've never seen anything before that gave me, a white male, such a glimpse of how it feels to be working from 'down'. It was shattering. But for me, like the workshop, it passed.

At 10 in the evening it was 'Schindler's List'. I saw the film when it came out in 1993, the late show in a Hampstead cinema with a significantly Jewish audience. And it, too, was shattering. Easter followed and, while I was travelling through France, I saw news of the Hebron massacre. Staying in the mountains in southern France I felt, it seemed, hypersensitive to this three-sided monotheistic crush I'd been following since I first came to Israel when I was 18. In France I dreamed a dream that prefigured my own conversion to Islam and, in some way, it explains the big 'why' that hangs over Israel and Palestine. In the dream I was driving a horse and cart around Stamford Hill, London's Orthodox Jewish area. It had been made a ghetto and I was transporting Jews around it. I then made a trip outside, with one Orthodox Jewish man. The streets outside were lined with people venting their rage against him. They were screaming, 'World War III against the Jews!' I felt for him and stopped at a roadside stall to buy him, of all things, a sticky bun. When I turned to buy the cake I left a man dressed entirely in black, fur hat, jacket, trousers. When I turned back to give him the cake he had become an Arab, dressed in sparkling white kaffiyeh and jalabiya. Transformation. My destiny? Theirs? Or both?

At the end of the film, Schindler is given a ring by the Jews he had saved, inscribed with a quotation from the Bible: 'He who saves a life, it is as if he saved the whole of humanity.' In the Qur'an we find the quotation: 'We decreed of the Children of Israel that whosoever killeth a human being for other than manslaughter or corruption in the earth, it shall be as if he killed all mankind, and whosoever saveth the life of one, it shall be as if he saveth the whole of mankind. Our messengers came unto them of old with clear proofs but Lo! Afterwards many of them became prodigals in the earth.' (5:32) We find this after the story of the two sons of Adam, known as Cain and Abel in the Bible. As sons of Adam they were indeed nearly the whole of mankind.

Another curious parallel is the term 'Musselman' that was used of long-term prisoners of the concentration camps. Though partly a joke on ‘muscle man’, the racist jibe aspect of the term alludes to a shared Semitic origin that branched after Abraham through his sons Ishmael and Is’haq (Isaac). Some Jewish and Muslim traditions see part of the significance of Abraham being that he was the only believer, *hanif*, in the world. Yet he still submitted to the divine command to sacrifice his son, thus to ‘kill all (believing) mankind.’

Jews and Muslims disagree about which son, but as even the Bible says (three times) ‘thine only son’ and given that, while the keynote of the sacrifice is submission, Isaac’s son Jacob (Yaacob) was renamed Israel, which means he who struggles with God in Hebrew, there is much that suggests Ishmael, to Muslims at least. It is my tentative contention that Jewish refusal to recognise this submission as the central aspect of faith and their taking up, in some way willingly, the opposite role of struggler with God, has been the burden they have lived under, and that this predisposition is *precisely why* they were chosen. It is not ‘better’, certainly not ‘blue-eyed’, but still true. Because if they can finally annihilate their ego, as many scholars figuratively interpret Abraham/Ibrahim’s sacrifice, then anyone can. And, insh’Allah, will.

In this interpretation, the ‘Musselmen’ of the concentration camps were brutally, inhumanly, forced to submit. Though ‘mortally wounded’, as Ehud Barak said in his Holocaust Remembrance Day speech, they rose from the ashes and came here. To Palestine. A miracle. But the greater miracle would surely be a voluntary submission. Here in the Holy Land.

When the Prophet Muhammad received his message, he encountered a Jewish community that was expecting a prophet, but assumed that it would be one of their own. Their pride, their refusal to submit to a divine opportunity that did not accord with their own expectations meant that only 39 converted at that time.

This time, Jewish conversion to Islam seems as unlikely, certainly as unexpected, but the question has to be asked, Why not? Though hardly a simple step, it would acknowledge the supreme transcendence of the unity of God, His ultimately unknowable plan, and our appropriate relationship with him – submission. As muslims, musselmen. In an imagined conversation written in 1905 between the King of the Khazars and a rabbi, speaking the thoughts of Judah Halevi, the rabbi says, ‘If the majority of us, as you say, would learn humility toward God and His Law from our low station, Providence would not have forced us to bear it for such a long period. Only the smallest portion (of us) thinks this; the majority may expect reward, because they bear their degradation, partly from necessity, partly from their own free will…. If we bear our exile and degradation for God's sake, as is meet, we shall be the pride of the generation which will come with the Messiah, and accelerate the day of deliverance we hope for.'

In this sense, the Holocaust was not a punishment, as some call it (even some Jews), but a sacrifice. Isaac was sacrificed, over 6 million times, but his son has survived, as Israel, and has since then indeed struggled with God. If obedience, submission to God, the dominant theme of the Bible, were finally accomplished in this day, not for the sake of the Palestinians, nor the Muslims, nor peace, nor even for the sake of the Jews, but for the sake of God, then surely from thence blessings would truly fall on all humanity.

23rd November.

39 days to go. I know because a big electronic Coca-Cola hoarding in the centre of Ramallah tells me so. Later I read in a Nablus mosque that if you read Coca-Cola in a mirror - how do people discover these things? - it reads 'La Muhammad, La Makkah', 'No Muhammad, No Makkah'. Me, I'm totally in favour of anything that discourages Coke consumption but I'm not sure that was the main point. I think it was more like 'They're getting at us again.' And actually what it seems to read is 'Li Muhammad, Li Makkah'. 'Li' means 'to', so it's positive. So we should drink more?

24th Nov. (-38)

...But what really concerns me most at the moment is not Coke but water. It is not raining here. At an interfaith meeting in Tiberias next to the Galilee a group that includes the mufti of Ramallah, the Dalai Lama, bishops and rabbis, prays for rain. The rabbi directs them south to pray, the direction of both Jerusalem and Makkah, he said. The Dalai Lama went along with it, saying that he didn't think it would do any good, but it wouldn't do any harm. But it rained. Though mainly it blew. Something got through. Both ways. But not enough.

28th Nov. (-34)

The arrest of the Manifesto 20 sparks a fist-fight between pro- and anti- PNA (Palestinian National Authority) students. The PNA is accused of creating a culture where corruption can flourish. It is pre-exam time and I try to link this point to the culture of cheating which pervades student life here, amply aided by one-word answer and multiple choice exams. I tell them it is against the rules; it is *haram,* forbidden, and it destroys any sense of independence and trust in your own opinions. 'We know,' they say, like we're all just saying what we have to say. But two Ahmeds laugh when I say the word 'Haram'. Later comments show them to be of the Islam-holds-us-back school of thought (from setting up beer factories to be precise). I don't even mind that but within minutes of the start of the gap-fill listening exam they're both writing 'less than <u>un</u> inch' and 'I just woke up from a <u>north</u>.' When I tell them about this I say that if they want to dump their religion then they need to have something else. Sometimes here it seems that a few moral exhortations are enough to bring people back to the straight and narrow. At times like this I despair. Later I wonder if it's my business to feel so RESPONSIBLE.

10th Dec. (-22)
The weather has been bitterly cold for 2 weeks. But no rain.

13th Dec. (-19)
Sometimes it's easy to forget the political situation, the 'bigger picture.' How much it excuses, *Allah alim*, God knows. Israeli undercover soldiers 'liquidate' Iyad Battat, a Hamas member, and Nadir Masalma. They shot at the house for 3 hours after the target had been shot in the street. Meanwhile, the mother and children hid in the bathroom until the soldiers dragged them out. They made the children and the wounded strip naked 'for security reasons' then led them handcuffed past the dead and wounded through the streets. 'Luck was on the side of the good guys this time' one of the officers said. 'Revenge' said Israeli daily Ma'ariv. Hebrew for 'Gotcha!'? Another, Ha'aretz, talked about the 'dark side' of this 'relative success', saying: 'The firing of anti-tank missiles in a situation in which children are present, comes perilously close to the methods terrorists use in their war against us.'

14th Dec. (-18)
One of those days when the hot, dry breeze seems to whip the moisture from your mouth, from the ground. Fasting, (it's Ramadhan) we move like desiccated creatures.

15th Dec. (-17)
Read Abdul Hakim Murad's article on Allah's vengeance and the Turkish earthquake. Think about writing about that and rain here. But it rains. A bit.

17th Dec. (-16)
A weekend in England for my sister's wedding. Read A.N. Wilson in the Evening Standard: 'The next century will be dominated by the mullahs.' Faced with confusion and globalisation 'who will be able to resist... the instinctive belief of mankind: namely that there is some moral law outside ourselves, some mysterious power greater than ourselves?' The whole tone of the article reminded me of something that Richard Bach once wrote: what the caterpillar calls death, the

master calls a butterfly. In this vein, Wilson says: 'Islam has never failed. It has merely paused.' *SubhanAllah*, brothers and sisters. We are the butterflies of the future, waiting to flap our wings.

Being in Palestine, I sometimes wonder if the return of 'Isa, Jesus, who Muslims believe is Jewish, Messiah *and* a Prophet of Islam, will not somehow vindicate all the faiths, but in the context of an essential submission to Allah. I am a caterpillar trying to imagine...

...And being in England I wonder where I should really be. At one point I thought that the balance came down in favour of Palestine, but there is a roughness, stubbornness and a *jahiliya*-like ignorance here. A typical Palestinian day includes so many instances of petty dishonesty and thoughtlessness, the biggest example of the former being that people are like this only because of fifty years of occupation. I never quite bought the idea that it would be wonderful to live in a Muslim country because I was never convinced that such a thing existed in any large way. There are moments, fleeting communications, some people. There is prayer, in Al Aqsa and elsewhere, when my limited thoughts and imaginings are stilled. But...?

19th Dec. (-13)

On the flight back there are one or two possible Millennialists coming to test their Big Bang Theory. I read that lateral thinker Edward De Bono has been appointed as some sort of expert on the Middle East peace process. One of his first recommendations is Marmite. A zinc deficiency leads to tension. Marmite contains zinc. Apart from the idea of Marmite soldiers, I find this quite persuasive. My little jar is nearly empty. If anyone is passing...[8]

24th Dec. (-8)

Bethlehem. It rains heavily, here and elsewhere. Few foreigners at the Xmas celebrations. It is a strange Western re-export, this 2000th (plus) Christmas - lights on trees, Father Xmases, and spiritual music. The Palestinian press covers continuing land grabs by the Israelis while everyone else is watching the Syrian peace track and the Golan.

---

[8] On the basis of this article, someone did bring a big jar of Marmite, which I picked up from a shop in the Old City in Jerusalem.

27th Dec. (-5)

Cold and cloudy but no more rain. I meet a Palestinian who lived 18 years in the States before returning two years ago. He says: 'I'm not saying everyone here's bad. There must be some good people here. But where are they?'

29th Dec. (-3)

Zuhr, midday prayer, at Al Aqsa. I feel proud when the police tell me, 'No tourists!' and I tell them I've come to pray. I feel privileged. And the place never fails to impress me, the beauty, the harmony, yet the diversity of the design, so familiar yet new every time. I feel a tranquillity here I feel nowhere else. The people are gentler - some even return my Salaams. 'Its environs We have blessed,' it says in the Qur'an (17.1) Paradoxically it is, of course, the heart of the problem. And the key to the solution is, I believe, the ability, and willingness, to transcend this place, as the Prophet did literally in the Israa.

30th Dec. (-2)

The weather is warm again. The radio is speculating about the possible effects of the Y2K 'bug' and Christians trying to blow up Al Aqsa. Yesterday a Palestinian from Nazareth was caught there with an Uzi in his bag. A cash point machine swallowed my card.

31st Dec. (-1)

Jumaa at Al Aqsa. I'm zealously checked twice. After the normal prayer there is a special prayer for rain, yet the *wudhu* taps still gush. There are half a million people gathered. Some are overcome by the fasting, the heat and emotion during the rain prayer. Later I learn that more bombs were found today. In Bir Zeit someone finds a live four day-old baby by the rubbish bins.

On TV there are ripples of parties around the world. At midnight, Tel Aviv, visible from our balcony, becomes Beirut. Whizzes and bangs. Particularly bangs. But the New Millennium has arrived without anything worse. *Al hamdulillah.* Thank God.

1st Jan 2000. (0)

The smell of rain, an awful dream and a family argument that looks like our last straw. We came here with a question, Is it Allah's will that we stay? This Holy Land, Land of the Prophets and my wife's homeland. The place where I've clocked up over three years in the second half of my life. A friend said today that most people aren't Muslim here - it's not a birthright, it's something you live. It's the lack of concern about others and the extreme self-sensitivity, the repressed anger and frustration (which probably explains a lot of things). There's the education system's tolerance of cheating and its rigid, unquestioned 'western' style, the mess of the environment - more landfill than holy land, less bottle bank than West Bank. And the number of times I've been told something about pay, work conditions, services, costs, by employers, lawyers, landlords, taxi drivers, that amount to lies by the time doing anything about it comes... The voyeuristic videos and the muscular military music of the glorious Arab armies. The weakness of my Arabic which undermines my position as a man when I have to ask my wife to intercede. And the strain that puts on her. And somehow I wanted, and in a way still want, to live here. Because I still believe THIS PLACE IS IMPORTANT. And I actually like a lot of the people.

I read recently that we should always remember that when Saidna Muhammad began his Prophethood, the Arabs were drinkers, gamblers, they killed their daughters, they believed in many gods. They were drowning in their own ignorance, in *jahiliya.* Yet after 23 years they were disciplined, unified, purified and had laid the foundations for the world's greatest empire.

Which means only 8395 days to go...

4th Jan/27th Ramadhan.

The night they call Leilat Al Qadr here. The night the Qur'an came down. Tonight the heavens open and it came down rain.

11th Jan.

A quarter of last year's rain fell in two days. It virtually stopped for Eid, then started after. Yet people still find the idea of Allah somehow old-fashioned. I read a topical quote from that man Edward de Bono in his book 'The Use of Lateral Thinking':

'Sects which assemble on mountain tops on predicted days of doom to await the end of the world do not come down on the morrow shaken in their ideas, but with a renewed faith in the mercifulness of the Almighty.'

SALAAM MR CASPIE

(Letter to Ha'aretz)

I too find it a little hard to begin like this, but yes, it is a custom in Arabic too. (Have you noticed just how much we share?) Neither do I write too many letters like this but your letter has also left me, at least, a little indignant. I have mixed feelings about the recent riots but even the most liberal of Israelis, you are clearly one, miss something. Yes, you know all the 'excuses', yet you still don't understand the rage. And I think you should.

Firstly, no. The Palestinians did not experience, and are not experiencing, a 'Holocaust'. But they, more than half a whole nation, became refugees, an event perhaps unique in history. And one of the reasons for Palestinian rage is precisely BECAUSE their catastrophe was not as great as yours. Because it has always been compared, and has always come off as less compelling, less dramatic, less worthy of compassion, and has consequently been marginalised and frequently dismissed. And secondly, no you don't beat up Arabs on the Day of Remembrance, nor throw stones at the German Embassy, nor do the Japanese attack Americans on Hiroshima Day. Surely all those affected carry emotional scars from these events, but in all cases there has been some acknowledgement, some redress. This is patently not the case with the Palestinians' 'Nakba'. 'Those prohibited from returning to their former homes' number millions, and they are still suffering physically, emotionally and, since Oslo, increasingly, hopelessly. This is why there were so many of them on the streets on Al-Nakba Day.

They express and symbolise a Palestinian rage that is felt on many levels. Firstly, there is a rage against Israelis who obviously still oppress, who take land and build settlements, hold on to prisoners and the rest. The right, and the government which permits something like a state of apartheid to continue. But there is also rage against the 'left' in Israel, those who think Israel is already giving up so much, who point to actions like the 'dramatic' dismantling of the hilltop settlements as a sign of intent. More dramatic pictures on Channel 2 maybe, but at the end of the day, how many were really dismantled? How many were simply moved? And how many are still there? And what was going on in the existing settlements in the meantime? And how much more land was taken elsewhere, in the usual grinding, remorseless, undramatic way? Throughout the history of Zionism partial truths have been elevated to the status of whole truths. This is but one recent example.

Another is the furore around Abu Dis. Israelis speak of a united Jerusalem as if it was some sort of ideal. Giving up East Jerusalem as some sort of unthinkable act. But so what if you do give it up? The parts of the city that your government has not expropriated, 'cleansed' and Judaised are Palestinian, as Palestinian, as Arab, as it is possible to be, no matter what it says on the map or (ambiguously) in their residents' papers nor to whom they pay their exorbitant taxes. All this for the privilege of having to cram themselves into the Ministry of the Interior building if they want anything done, to be crowded into ever-shrinking areas and to be picked on or ignored in exact reverse proportion to what they might wish for. If you go to these places, East Jerusalem, Abu Dis, Hebron, where there are more Israeli flags than soldiers and more soldiers than residents, you will see, misquoting Weizmann or Herzl, that these places are as Jewish as England is Italian. All you are giving up is an idea, a shape of a map. And yet you expect gratitude. 'Is this the thanks we get?' as Tel Aviv's mayor said, for touting the possibility of 'returning' 20% of Mandated Palestine, this in the face of the continued 'creation of facts', and the numerous other 'undramatic' demolitions, expulsions, permits denied, water cut off, economic and trade restrictions and the rest.

Yes, people responded to the calls from the PNA. But Amira Hass writes of a man in Gaza saying: 'Don't think you are really seeing us. We are just a picture. Inside everything is empty.' This PNA is not really us. We know about the private bank accounts, the detentions and human rights abuses, and we see the petty arrogance of some of them in their blessed red number-plated cars. We don't really recognise ourselves in them, but we too elevate our partial truths into totalities, and they are all we can offer. When we look at the peace and our leaders and your leaders, we think, if this is so good, why does it feel so bad? Many Palestinians know that the Days of Rage were, in some part, a game, the game of who controls whom. In calling for the demonstrations the PNA were at once showing that they could control the people yet at the same time could not control the people if things got out of hand. It was a threat. An order to demonstrate is not 'a mathematical equation.' It might lead to 'unforeseen problems… popping up' such as a chain of action and reaction. 'We will initiate, but things may get out of hand, and we might not be able to control things.' This philosophy plays upon the very fact of a latent hostility to the PNA, but it deflects and obscures this rage by focusing it on the always more acceptable 'other'. Many of those who took to the street may have known in part that they were being used, but our greater anger is still reserved for you, the Israelis.

As we peel away these layers of rage we finally come to something you allude to. There is a rage that is felt towards the self, a sort of self-hatred and lack of 'desire to be happy' (and here too we are holding up a mirror for you to ask yourselves the same question). The Intifada years were not as glorious as they are sometimes painted. But there was an overriding sense of community engaged in some sort of united struggle for some sort of positive end. But between 1993 and 1999 the percentage of Palestinians not interested in politics rose from 11% to 41%. In that time, Palestinian society has come to reflect your own – materialistic, self-centred, irreligious and over-sexualised. We may complain bitterly about the PNA's corruption and abuse of power, though we know that in our heart of hearts we are not entirely without sin in these departments. So it is infinitely easier to cast the first stone than to look at ourselves and confront our own selves.

But these are ultimately not 'excuses'. In the end we both - you and us – in the heat of confrontation, need to look to ourselves and engage in what the Prophet Muhammad called the Greater Jihad, the struggle with our own egos. We cannot forget the Lesser Jihad, nor ultimately separate it entirely, but in some way we must deal with the self as if the 'other' did not exist. To do that we need some moments of peace for reflection and also the feeling that the other wishes us well in doing so. It is often said that it is rare or even unheard of for the more powerful party in such a conflict to yield its valuable assets, but this is a Holy Land and real peace here would surely be blessed. And the power to make it so is in your hands.

So give us a break, a break that would allow us to give you one without it seeming and feeling like it was some kind of capitulation. Stop grinding us down even as you say otherwise. See us as human beings in whom the divine spark still shines, not simply as a market to be exploited or a threat to your lives. Let us develop socially and economically without your petty, monstrous restrictions. Stop building and expanding settlements and expropriating land and property. Give equality of treatment and services to those you rule, in Israel and Jerusalem if indeed you value your unified country and capital so highly. Don't give our leaders the chance to be corrupt and duplicitous. Release the prisoners. Allocate resources, water particularly, fairly. Treat us with dignity and you will find respect.

It may surprise you that there is much about you that we admire, but from where we are, in your shadow, it is a partial truth and it is only your shadow we feel. It is cold and dark here, and only burning rage gives any light. So show some light unto the nations, if that's an idea you take seriously, and begin with us. Oslo and other papers are meaningless without it.

With all due respect, salaam aleikum.[9]

---

[9] Reply to: http://www.jewishpost.com/archives/news/israeli-left-wing-journalist-fed-up-with-arafat.html. First published: 26 April 2000

THE SIGNIFICANCE OF JERUSALEM

It is being called the Al-Quds Intifada and it has surprised lots of people, myself included, even though I have just come back from living in Palestine for a year. The fighting may begin to die down soon, and it may not, but conflagrations that relate to Al-Aqsa, the mosque at the heart of the Jerusalem issue, carry the potential within them to become truly apocalyptic. Hizbullah kidnappings on the Israeli-Lebanese border, attacks on Americans in Yemen, oil price rises and demonstrations all over the Muslim world have carried hints of this, of what might be or might yet be.

Hadith concerning the Last Days say that there will be a battle between the Muslims and the Jews, that the anti-Christ (*a-Dajjal*) will come, that 'Isa (Jesus) will descend to Syria and come to Jerusalem where he will pray the morning prayer and then he will kill the *Dajjal* at Lydda (Lod). These beliefs, and the very sanctity of Masjid Al-Aqsa because of its history and because of the Prophet's ascension to heaven from there, mean that no matter how controversial issues of borders, settlements, water and refugees are, it is the final status of Jerusalem that has the power to drive Palestinians onto the street to risk death or serious injury (which is what the innocuously sounding 'wounded' often carry for the rest of their lives). In the end, the sanctity of Jerusalem cannot be compromised. Reminding us of Suleyman's judgement concerning the disputed child, cutting in half, or compromise, is not an option.

This does not mean that I am in favour of the 'undivided, eternal Jerusalem' that the Israelis say they believe in. Rather, it is that the judgement to 'divide the child' should ask us to reflect on exactly where we stand in our relationship with God, or rather, 'who really owns the baby'?

Jerusalem reduces the people in this world to two kinds. There are those who acknowledge a greater power in this universe than our selves and submit to it, and those who do not. Arguably the first group includes at least some Christians and Jews but it is we Muslims alone who actually define our *deen*, our faith, in terms of this relationship – Islam means submission while Christianity is primarily focused on Christ's role as intermediary between God and humanity, and Judaism is primarily focused on the Jews' own 'Chosen' position between God and humanity.

Thus, where the first group is the 'Muslim' group, the second is… what? It includes some Muslims for sure, some Christians, atheists, agnostics, some who are committed members of it, some who are there by default, some who go through life with 'a sense of something' rather than a belief in anything. And so on. What they have in common is a refusal to submit to an absolute divine authority. And there is one group whose name means 'he who struggles with God', who have been sent a succession of Prophets to bring them back to the rightful path and who even acknowledge that it is their own (non-specific) guilt that has been a cause for punishment in history. In the Bible, Israel was the name that the man/angel/God gave Jacob after the two fought through the night, and Judah was Israel's son through whom the line survived. It is in this sense that I think that the Jewish people have been Chosen. They embody something in their spirit that IS quintessentially human, and that is a tendency, a profound tendency, to resist submission to God. It is, in a way, an admirable quality until the point where its expression is at the expense of other people. And in the first two weeks of the Al-Quds Intifada alone the tally was over 90 dead and 1000 wounded. Since 1948 it numbers thousands.

If the Jews, the symbols of the group who 'struggle with God', have been Chosen by God, it begs questions as to how this has manifested in our time and why. The 'how', I would argue, is through the instrument of the Holocaust. Just as in the Bible the kingdom of Israel was destroyed for its sins by the Assyrians who were in turn destroyed for theirs, so too the Jews were murdered in their millions by the Nazis who were then destroyed. The 'why' is controversial and relates to both what came before and what came, and will come insh'Allah, after. Before, there was not simply the Jewish rejection of God through assimilation but also the avowedly secular movement to 'force the end', a Jewish term that denotes acts that are specifically designed to bring about the Final Confrontation. This movement was, and has been, Zionism. The punishment, the sacrifice, the reward and the opportunity were the equally inseparable facts of the Holocaust and the birth of Israel. The result of this was the reunion of the Jewish people with the land of their ancestors and the opportunity to fulfil God's plan on earth. The question is, what is that? It could not be exactly to pick up where they had left off because, in the meantime, history had moved on, even if it had effectively ‘ended’ for Jews after the expulsion from the land by the Romans in the 1st Century AD.

As far as humanity was concerned, its relationship with its Creator had not stood still. Christianity, in a sense, took the limited Jewish direct relationship with the One Universal God and made it a universal option, though the hallmark centrality of intermediaries, whether Jesus, Pope or priest, made it, in Muslim eyes at least, ultimately flawed. Then Islam was revealed and, until 1918, was the dominant power and influence over the land where definitions of monotheism get thrashed out. And it was these monotheists, Christians and Muslims, whom the Jews faced when they returned to Palestine, when they indeed did return to the land of their fathers. The land had changed. Palestine now contained places that were not only associated with the birth of Christianity but also one place that Muslims regard as the third holiest place in the world, the place that represented the transcendental unity of God. The Jews, or some of them, see it as the site of the Third Temple, following Solomon’s and Herod’s. Muslims believe that that temple has, as even the Israeli Tourist Board ‘kind of’ said in its millennium adverts last year, already been built. And yet the question as to precisely why God might have done all this seems to have gone, if not unasked, at least unanswered by Israelis.

Like no other place in the world, this is the question that Jerusalem asks. Since I first went to Israel more than half my life ago to work on a kibbutz I feel that I have been peeling back layers of an onion or perhaps removing the veils of my own delusion. I don’t imagine I have arrived at the centre, at wisdom, at enlightenment but at some point I crossed a line. I struggled for years with a search for God, for the meaning of God in my life. It was often painful, but I did it on my own terms, hence my slightly grudging-sounding respect for Israelis and also my profound sympathy for the pain they, as Jews, have suffered historically. For years I viewed Islam as too restrictive and too, I suppose, pessimistic about human nature. At some point though, I translated the word ‘restriction’ into ‘stability’, and ‘pessimistic’ into ‘realistic’ and in doing so found whole new vistas within the word ‘freedom’ and ‘happiness’. That, I believe, is the opportunity that faces Jewish Israelis, and indeed everyone. But something stops people identifying this by no means self-evident truth.

People feel sorry for Palestinians, slightly more so than they used to, and rather more when they see the kind of brutality that has been on view in Jerusalem, the West Bank and Gaza in recent weeks. But it fades, and the effectively pro-Israel status quo holds again, particularly after some Palestinian atrocity. The reason is that in the end, most Christians, nominally or otherwise, do not identify themselves with the stone-throwing youths who are willing to die for their beliefs. They identify far more with the powerful, western-looking army and people that opposes them with all their God-given power. It is a power that seems both a puzzle and encumbrance, but they, the Israelis as much as the West, are loath to question or do without it, because ultimately they believe they deserve it. And for Christians, being used to intermediaries in their relationship with God and having discarded, usually, the Pope, priests, and very often Jesus as well, the fall-back option is the people from whom Jesus came. The Jews. And there is, of course, the appalling guilt about the Holocaust.

The Holocaust in some way legitimises excesses that, if committed by Palestinians, would be totally unacceptable. The death of a Rabbi recalls the millions killed in Auschwitz. A child killed is another Anne Frank. As I write, on the evening of the lynching death of the Israeli soldiers in Ramallah and the ensuing rocket attacks, I am reminded of the voices of Israeli soldiers who served in Lebanon when faced with Arab atrocities, worse than this, and their pride that they weren't reduced to that level. And I thought then, and think now, of statistics and ballistics. The Israelis killed more Palestinians in one day of bombing of Beirut than the number of Israelis who had been killed by Palestinian terror since 1948. And every death was as devastating for the Palestinians as for the Israelis but with a difference. When you unleash a rocket, a mortar shell, you do not feel it or see the results of your action. You are cold, and you are certainly no 'barbarian'. And you do not see the seeds of rage you sow. So people are surprised when the harvest is reaped when Ariel Sharon, coordinator of the Sabra-Shatilla Palestinian refugee camp massacres in Lebanon in 1982, prospective new Israeli Prime Minister, 'hard cop' to Barak's 'soft cop', visits Al-Aqsa to stake the eternal Jewish claim to the site. In the home-straight of the Peace Process we saw a glimpse of the always-suspect final settlement at Camp David. Then we saw Ariel Sharon on the finishing line that Thursday.

People are saying, why did you throw the peace away? Why the rage? It's just a few extremists who spoil it for the majority of good folk in the centre who just want to live in peace. And they say that it's not about religion, but about propaganda, or politics, or factions, or tribes, or money. But tell them it's not. It's about God and it's about religion. And religion means how you relate to God. Then ask them, nicely, and if it's appropriate, which side are you on?

GOING RIGHT, BEING RIGHT

Hilary Andersson on the BBC one morning before the election was neither the first nor the last to take the position, but she seems to typify it. The edge to the voice. The implied, How stupid the Palestinians are. It was by then very clear that Sharon was going to win and that he was going to be far less accommodating with the Palestinians than Barak. Yet the Palestinians were still making life difficult for the latter, persisting with violence and rejecting the 'best-ever', last chance he was offering. It was the Palestinians' fault.

September and the beginning of the Al-Aqsa Intifada was not the result of a peace process that had revealed its true colours (mostly white and blue, though with a few red stripes) at Camp David in July, nor a response to an Israeli citizen (and 'backers', a thousand or so) simply exercising a religious right to visit Judaism's holiest place and mentioning, in passing, that it was never going to be anything but. No! Again, it was the Palestinians' refusal to compromise and their genetic allergy to peace.

And while we're at it, none of this would be a problem if, just as Piglet so generously did in 'Pooh and the Blustery Day', the Palestinians had simply agreed to go and live somewhere else fifty years ago. (By the way, owl lost his house in a storm, Eeyore found a suitable alternative – Piglet's place, Pooh offered to house-share with Piglet, and Christopher Robin threw a party for the heroes. To decode the parable, simply substitute Israel, Britain, Palestine, Jordan and the US). And the book had obviously not been translated into Arabic because none of the other Arab states let the Palestinians house-share. The Palestinians (and Arabs) again.

As none of the right things have happened, the Israelis have *still* not found peace, and have been *forced* to behave in a way that is against their very natures, to cope with the situation. Only regular publications of books and articles about how the Jews invented human rights in the Bible and after consoles them.

In the Guardian, post-election, champion of the Israeli Peace Now movement, Amos Oz, calls Sharon 'Arafat's gift to Israel', blaming Arafat for rejecting Camp David, a jibe that David Grossman, usually a challenger of Zionist orthodoxies, repeats.

A British-born Israeli couple, 'ordinary voters' who voted for Barak last time, voted for Sharon because 'there is no hope of peace because the Palestinians do not want it.' And they are, of course, in their eyes at least, right.

What we have here, now, and what it means, is something to do with facts, a lot to do with faiths, and even more to do with faith. And everything to do with fate.

Israel has been creating some of the facts for years, in the form of settlements - they even coined the term 'creating facts' to describe the process – and their rate of expansion increased dramatically under the peacenik Barak whose landslide removed hawkish Bibi Netanyahu. These settlements, so 'material', so visible – not notional or emotional – were proof enough that the Israelis were acting in bad faith. It would have been hard, but the Israeli government could have started moving them after Baruch Goldstein's Hebron Massacre or Barak's 'Peace' victory. But nothing happened. Instead they have expanded, and elsewhere there have been the 'feelings', the hints, the not-very-dramatic-on-TV actions by Israelis, roadblocks, legalism, permits, demolitions, that suggest that they do not want any Palestinian industry, agriculture, tourism, state, anything, to survive, let alone thrive, at Israel's expense or otherwise.

Then there are the facts of Camp David. Oz lists the things that Arafat rejected: a Palestinian state with 'minor border modifications' (some said 92, 93, 95% of the original) and East Jerusalem as its capital, Temple Mount under Islamic protection. Amira Hass, another critical Israeli journalist, points out that both Israeli and Palestinian towns on the West Bank occupy about 8% of the land each and the Israeli ones would still have had their road access. A contiguous Palestinian state would have been out of the question. And after taking into account buffer zones, 'rented' areas (in Hebron), land under the Dead Sea and the land annexed to Jerusalem, as Robert Fisk says, the Palestinians were looking at bits of land, amounting to 60ish % of the West Bank with a bit of sand next to the Gaza Strip thrown in. Jerusalem would have been garbage and terrorist collection and 'control' of the surface of the mosques. (The re-emergence of the refugees, another key area, may in fact be telling in explaining why the Israelis have reacted so unsympathetically to Arafat being 'led' by events. He has been forced, here and elsewhere, to both clarify and raise his bottom line, and that, to Israel is unacceptable.)

What is striking here, and has always been striking, is the Israeli wilfulness to believe what serves them on an egotistical level. This usually involves raising an element of truth to a totality, and this leads to a certain amount of self-fulfilling prophecy. As in responses to the Peace Process (and how little the Palestinians want peace, particularly), facts can be marshalled to serve 'being right', but that does not necessarily mean being correct. There was an implicit, and sometimes explicit, recognition of this Jewish tendency in the Jewish acceptance of exile 2000 years ago as punishment for arrogance in the land. Returning to it now, and vindicating, it seems, political Zionism, is both self-fulfilling prophecy and raising an element of truth to a whole, because while Jews were arguably the only monotheists 2000 years ago (Christians weren't a fully distinct group at the time of the destruction of Jerusalem), Jews are now a minority religion among three. However, they still implicitly claim to have the *only* authentic relationship with God, a claim also implicitly recognised by some Christians, and one that renders ours, in Jewish eyes, irrelevant. As things are, they have the power to make that message very clear and are likely to do so in the period following the election, whatever Palestinians do.

As that *is* the case, this faith, Judaism in its Israeli form, can only be met by Faith, in the sense of *iman*. It is very difficult to see what can make life more bearable in Palestine than a stronger *iman*, and the sending of prayers and material support from outside for the people who are suffering is probably the best we can do. It can feel a little trite to say it, but Allah only tests us to the capacity that we can bear. Also, hadith testify to the fact that the people of that place are some of the finest and will be some of the few who have kept faith at the time of the coming of the End Day. They deserve, and need, our support.

What will happen next, what Fate will bring, Allah alone knows. There needs to be some seismic shift of consciousness among Israelis at least for something like Jeff Siddiqui's 'Liberty and Justice for all' to occur (see last issue of Q-News). There could be a war. Or it could go on like this for years. Personally I'm praying for a conversion of the people of Israel to Islam, though hearts may be too hard for that at the moment. Words of the Prophet, peace be upon him, suggest that it is not actually worth struggling for a political, temporal, societal solution to our problems, because every generation will get worse, until the final days. So maybe the best that can be done for Palestine is prayer and charity and locating our *jihad* internally, in our lives. For Palestine, these words to the Children of Israel in the Qur'an may offer hope:

'Your Lord may well show mercy to you, but if you revert to your evil behaviour, We shall revert to chastising you.' (17:8)

BAD RELATIONS? - Muslims & Jews – Part 1

2001 ended and 2002 began with a still-running debate in the press about the resurgence of anti-Semitism. Since then, events in Palestine have deteriorated to an all-time low, and threaten now to spin out of control. With this in mind I have tried to write about the nature of Muslim-Jewish relations in a way that considers the past, present and future of this relationship. Insh'Allah, I intend to find some kind of still point from which to view something around which the whole future of the world is likely to turn. So, what do we think of the Jews? And what should we?

Attacks on Muslims, both verbal and physical, have increased since 11th September, as we all know. They have also increased on Jews and though the apparent spur is the situation in Palestine, many feel that the issue is often merely thinly veiled anti-Semitism, whether from Muslims or non-Muslims. For Muslims, many of us also Semitic, if it's the former, is it legitimate? And if the latter, should we be pleased?? Should we be pleased when the French ambassador calls Israel 'a s****y little country' and asks, 'Why should we be in danger of World War Three because of these people?' Are the Jews our 'natural' enemy? If so, is my enemy's enemy my friend? And how are we supposed to relate to 'these people'? And how, indeed, are we related?

The Legacy of the Prophets

To answer the last first, we are related through Ibrahim, or Abraham – Muslims through the line of Isma'il, and Jews (and therefore Christians) through Isaac (Is'haq). We share the belief in the intended sacrifice of the son, though we (Muslims) generally believe the son was Isma'il and the place Makkah. Jews and Christians believe it was Is'haq in Jerusalem, a view that tends to predominate in 'neutral' discourse on the matter.

As Muslims we believe that Ibrahim was 'not a Jew, nor a Christian but he was a *hanif* (an upright person who believes in God) and a Muslim.' (3:67) This is probably best understood in terms of practice based on *fitra* – the natural religiosity of human beings whereby we are disposed to submit to the absolute authority of God (the literal meaning of Muslim), rather than in terms of Islamic practice in the form perfected by the Prophet Muhammad. (Much inter-faith dialogue seems to break down at this point. In the same way, **we** know what we mean when we talk about reverting to Islam, but the term only succeeds in alienating non-Muslim listeners.) What we believe is that Islam was the original, the primordial religion, and all nations since have been sent prophets to guide them back to it. We are of the same Semitic family, and also we share many of the same Prophets. In our understanding, Islam is not Jewish in origin, the standard Orientalist position. Rather, Judaism is islamic (rather than *I*slamic) in origin.

Because of all this, we are closer to Judaism than any other faith. We believe that Jews were given special favour by Allah (2:47; Q2:122) but we believe that this was, or is, conditional on them behaving with justice, and that the Jewish role of being bearers of monotheism is now open to all. Our respective names are Islam, which means submission to God, and Israel, which, in Hebrew, means to struggle with God (and in Arabic to be slave of God). These may tell us something profound, but they do not give a licence of destruction to either for sins in the nature of that belief. In other words, Jews should not be punished for being Jews any more than Muslims should be punished for being Muslims - the punishment for wrong belief will ultimately be Allah's.

The Era of Jahaliya

Nonetheless, divine punishment for misdemeanours on earth carried out by human agents is an accepted notion. For the Jews, the second of these chastisements in this life was the destruction of the second temple by the Romans in 70CE (AD), following which the Jews were scattered around the Mediterranean area. In Arabia, they established large communities in the area of Madina where they eventually came to occupy a position of power, though by the time of the Prophet Muhammad they were more like a balance of power between the tribes of the Aws and the Khazraj. There were no Jews living in Makkah but the Ka'ba was venerated by Jews as an outlying Temple that had been raised by Abraham. That they had migrated to Arabia could be perceived as no accident – the Bible contains many prophecies that say a Prophet would come from there. One notable Jew, Al-Hayyaban, migrated from the relative luxury of Syria to Madina precisely because of this but died at the time of the Prophet's first revelation. He said, 'His hour is close upon you. Be ye the first to reach him, O Jews; for he will be sent to shed blood and to take captive the women and the children of those who oppose him. Let that not hold you back from him.'

The Era of the Prophet

However, the majority of Jews expected that the coming prophet would be a Jew. Bahira, a learned Christian who recognised Saidna Muhammad's prophethood before it had been revealed, warned him specifically that the Jews would be against him, a warning that was mostly accurate.

Once the Prophet began his call to Islam, the attitude of the Jews can be described as 'in favour of the message but against the messenger', as Martin Lings puts it in his *Seera* (Life) of the Prophet. When the dominant tribe in Makka, the Quraysh, asked the Jews of Yathrib (Madina) what they, having knowledge of Scripture and Prophets, thought of the veracity of the Prophet's message, the rabbis told them to ask three questions. 'If he tell you of them, then he is a Prophet sent by God.' The questions concerned the young men who left their lands in days of old and what happened to them; the traveller who went east and west to the ends of the earth; and the Spirit, and its nature. Though the Prophet was able to answer the questions through revelation, many still did not believe him. Or rather, they *would* not.

This became increasingly clear as time passed. During the Prophet's life, it has been calculated that only 39 Jews actually embraced Islam. One of these was Safiyya, the wife of Kinanah. She was a pious woman who was offered freedom or marriage to the Prophet after her husband was killed at the Battle of Khaybar. She chose the latter. One of the reasons for this was that she had overheard her husband and another of the Jews of Khaybar, Huyay, talking about the Prophet before meeting him, saying that he could not be what he said he was. On their return they had been deeply troubled, because they had realised that he *was* a Prophet, though their opposition did not cease.

Another Jewish outward denial of this truth was when Abu Sufyan of the Quraysh met with Jewish leaders actually within the Ka'ba and asked them which group they believed had the better religion, *deen*. The Jews said, in that holy place: 'You Quraysh have the better *deen*.'

It was not that the Prophet did not know all this. Nonetheless, in Madina at the start he established a covenant with the Jews of mutual loyalty and protection. The two faiths had equal status, Jews would only be required to follow their own laws and there was no requirement of them to recognise the prophethood of Saidna Muhammad. They were taken at their word. 'If they incline to peace, then make peace with them and put your trust in Allah,' (8:61), an injunction that still stands. It was only if they acted against the Muslims that they would face the consequences.

One Jewish group chose to do this. After the Muslims' victory at Badr they taunted the Prophet that had he been fighting real warriors (i.e. them) he would not have been so successful. The Prophet walked out. A few days later, an argument between a Muslim and a Jew in the market that led to deaths on both sides could have been arbitrated by the Prophet under the terms of the covenant. However, the Jews chose to make a fight of it and withdrew to fortified positions, sure that their skills and the promised reinforcements would be more than adequate to dispose of the Muslims. However, no reinforcements came and eventually they surrendered unconditionally. It is important to note that despite the Qur'anic injunction: 'If thou overcomest them in war, then make of them an example, to strike fear into those that are behind them, that they may take heed,' (8:57), the Jews were only banished rather than killed.

The Prophet's approach to the Jews can be seen as one of patience in the face of hostile thought, and action in the face of hostile acts. Typifying this was the killing he ordered of Ka'b ibn al-Ashraf, a poet who satirised the Prophet and called on the Quraysh to take revenge for Badr. When the Jews of the Bani Nadir tribe complained to the Prophet, he said: 'If he had remained as others of like opinion remain, he would not have been killed by guile.' He then invited the Jews to make a special treaty in addition to the covenant, which they did, though a later plan to murder him led to declaration of war, siege, surrender and their banishment. Under the terms of the treaty, the Jews were only allowed to keep what their camels could carry, but with the camels in single file and their curtains thrown open to reveal the enormity of their owners' wealth, the Jews marched out to the tune of fife and drum. Such arrogance was noted, as was the potential booty should defeat catch up with the Jews again.

A further campaign was launched by the Jews and Quraysh which was stopped at the Battle of the Trench. Following this, the Bani Qurayzah, a Jewish clan, was besieged by the Muslims and finally surrendered. They were offered Islam and five accepted, three having known Al-Hayyaban in their childhoods. The Prophet was sent a deputation by the clan of Aws asking for mercy for these Jews who were former allies. 'Will it satisfy you, men of Aws, if one of yourselves pronounce judgement on them?' he asked, and they agreed. Sa'd ibn Mu'adh, their chief, was appointed and he decreed that the men should be slain for breaking the treaty, to which the Prophet said: 'Thou hast judged with the judgement of God from above the seven heavens.' Huyay, one of the seven hundred to die, said to the Prophet before his death: 'I blame not myself for having opposed thee, but whoso forsaketh God, the same shall be forsaken', which is perhaps a way of saying that in the eyes of God either you or we are wrong.

It is important to notice that, though stern retribution is permitted, it was rarely the choice of the Messenger and that in this instance there was a clear opportunity for mercy to be claimed. Similarly, in another instance of action taken against the life of the Prophet when magic was used by Labid, a Jewish resident of Madina (undone, literally, by the recitation of the last two Suras of the Qur'an) no action was taken. Nor was any taken against the Jewish woman who poisoned the Prophet after the Muslim victory at Khaybar, which was the last confrontation between the Muslims and Jews in Arabia.

Khaybar itself contains many of the features of other Muslim-Jewish confrontations in that the Jews were numerically superior and confident of winning – their fortifications at Khaybar were proverbially impregnable. However, they were disunited and were let down by promised reinforcements. As the Qur'an says: 'Ill feeling is rife amongst them. Thou countest them as one whole, but their hearts are divided.' (59:14) The Muslims fought 'in ranks as if they were a close-built block' (61:4) and took one fortress after another. In defeat it was agreed that the Jews would go into exile – again there was no slaughter – but this time they would leave without possessions (remembering the over-proud display of before). The Prophet added the further clause that anyone found trying to do so would be put to death. Kinanah, the Jewish leader agreed.

It seems that the prevailing attitude among the Jews was that they were beaten and that the Prophet really was who he said he was. However, they insisted on only following Moses and the Torah, and the Prophet supported them in doing so. Nonetheless, the leader of the Jews, Kinanah, insisted in trying to conceal his riches, angrily dismissing counsel not to from his own people. Given that he had established those seven years before that he was not dealing with a normal adversary, this seems to be a suicidal form of pride and indeed he was discovered and executed.

Following Khaybar, the Prophet allowed some of the Jewish date farmers to stay, on the understanding that if he later ordered them to leave, they would do so (which, in fact, he did). Two further Jewish settlements of Fadak and Wadi l-Qura, which had been in league with Khaybar, were also sent into exile, but following Tabuk, the Prophet made a treaty with Jewish and Christian settlements to the north of Arabia in the Aqaba region that gave them protection.

This final act shows that there was no policy of hostility, nor any implacable malice, in the Prophet's treatment of the Jews. As far as events of that time went, the Jews were enemies as long as they behaved as such. The enmity was towards their crimes or actions, not towards their religion.

The Era of Muslim Ascendancy

This policy really explains why Jews were able to live and often thrive under Muslim rule until as recently as the modern age. None of the doings of the Bani Nadir or Kinanah were held against Jews, to the point where the stories are not particularly well-known. It is true that it wasn't a Golden Era for all everywhere, though the Jews were never felt as a disconfirming presence as was often the case in relations with Christians. On the contrary, they were often able to thrive as a religious community, following their own religious laws administered by their own judges, under the protection of Muslim government. This was particularly so in Iraq initially, and later in Cairo, Kairouan in Tunisia and in Muslim Spain. Maimonides, born in Spain and later resident of Cairo, was one of the greatest Jewish thinkers in history as well as being the doctor of Salah E-Din.

However, the coming of the modern era, the rise of nationalism and finally the State of Israel, would change everything.

'Holy is He Who carried His servant by night from the Holy Mosque (in Makkah) to the Farthest Mosque (in Jerusalem) – whose surroundings We have blessed – that We might show him some of Our signs. Indeed, He alone is All-Hearing, All Seeing.

'We gave Moses the Book, and made it a source of guidance for the Children of Israel, commanding: 'Take no other guardian beside Me.'

'You are the descendants of those We carried (in the Ark) with Noah. He was truly a thankful servant.

'Then We clearly declared to the Children of Israel in the Book: 'Twice you will work corruption in the earth and will act with great arrogance.' So, when the time for the fulfilment of the first prophecy drew near, We raised against you some of Our servants who were full of might, and they ran over the whole of your land. This was a prophecy verily fulfilled.

'Then we granted you an upper hand against them, and strengthened you with wealth and children, and multiplied your numbers. Whenever you did good, it was to your own advantage; and whenever you committed evil, it was to your own disadvantage. So, when the time of the second prophecy drew near We raised other enemies that would disfigure your faces and enter the Temple as they had done the first time, and destroy whatever they could lay their hands on.

'Your Lord may well show mercy to you, but if you revert to your evil behaviour, We shall revert to chastising you. We have made Hell a prison for those who are thankless of Allah's bounties.'

(The Qur'an, 17:1-8, Bani Isra'il – The Children of Israel)

In the previous chapter, I considered the historical relationship between Muslims and Jews until the establishment of the State of Israel in 1948. Though not always as idyllic as is sometimes claimed, while Jews had no political or national aspirations, they were treated as a protected community (*dhimmi*) and often thrived in freedom and security. As in the time of the Prophet, though Judaism was not to be regarded as a valid universal alternative, there was no obligation to accept Islam and communities were allowed to administer their own religious laws internally. Essentially, a particularist faith, Judaism, which believed in One God, existed under a universal faith, Islam, that believed in the same God, if not in the same way.

With the establishment of Israel, although the most obvious sort of change has been political, there has also been enormous religious change. Just as Jews have found it hard to reconcile *their* sense of themselves as a chosen people with the sufferings of the Holocaust, we Muslims have struggled to come to terms with *our* lack of success as witnesses to and bearers of Allah's chosen religion. Nowhere is this more keenly felt than in Palestine, where Jews have been given some redress for their sufferings at the cost of further suffering for Palestinians. In that place at least, the relationship between Judaism and Islam has shifted violently from coexistence between two different, though related, beliefs to competition between two apparently disconfirming beliefs, exacerbated by being over one piece of land that is sacred to both.

This relationship with the Jews as a political and powerful party in Palestine/Israel is one that is entirely new and the only comfort we can draw from it is that some hadith of the Prophet concerning the Jews and the Final Days do not make sense except in the context of a revived Israel, a fact that was starkly improbable during the Prophet's time. What this seems to suggest is that there is something intrinsic in the issue of the truth of religion not being resolved until the return of the Jews to the Holy Land. This fact of life, of faith, present at the time of the struggles between Jews and Muslims at the time of the Prophet but never fully played out, simply 'hid' after, under layers of history, until it was ready to emerge.

When talking of the final days, the Prophet made a number of predictions concerning the Jews that, in the context of the struggle he was engaged in with them in Arabia, sound, not hateful as some assume, but simply prophetic. Most often quoted is the Hadith that: 'The last hour will not come until the Muslims fight against the Jews and the Muslims kill them until the Jews will hide themselves behind a stone or a tree and the stone or tree will say, 'Muslim there is a Jew behind me. Come and kill him'.' This fight will take place in the Holy Land and will culminate in the fight between Jesus and the anti-Christ, the *Dajjal*, at Lydda, or Lod, the site of Ben Gurion airport.

Another Hadith says that there will be degeneration among Muslims that will see them following the ways of Jews and Christians, while another says that Jews, Christians and Muslims will all break up into 71, 72 and 73 sects respectively before the Final Days and that all but one sect of each group will go to paradise. The Muslim group that goes to Paradise will contain a large number of Muslims - we are not told of the size of the Jewish and Christian groups. A further Hadith says that the best of people will be found in the land of Palestine.

Taken as a whole, and particularly the last, it seems that something of this spirit sustains Palestinians facing the oppressive power of the Israeli army. Sometimes, though, it seems that though the inspiration of Palestinians may be religious, their aspiration is essentially national, the end being a nation either in the West Bank and Gaza Strip or in the whole of Palestine. The weakness of this position seems to be that it often does not consider this enemy and the uniqueness of this situation. We are dealing with a people who have a Sura in the Qur'an named after them, who have had almost all the Prophets we know the names of sent to them and who we also regard as the Chosen People. This begs questions like, How should we deal with them? And, Chosen for what? The answer to the second question may suggest a strategy for the first.

My understanding begins with the naming of Jacob as Israel, which means he who struggles with God, and follows that theme, through Moses calling his people 'stiff-necked', and the two expulsions from the Promised Land for not submitting to the laws of God, leading to exile and persecution. If one believes that God's laws are natural laws, as Muslims do, and that the appropriate response to those laws is willing submission, then it follows that to struggle with those laws is to, at best, expect no divine sustenance and at worst, to invite disaster. (I believe there is a subtle distinction between this and the idea of 'incurring divine punishment'). Such a position often gets its comeuppance in this life and, as I read on my first trip to Israel in 1981, 'the Jews are just like everyone else, only more so.'

In saying this I do not mean to simply blame the victim, or exonerate the Nazis or even the Assyrians of the Bible, but rather to say that people did God's will. To put it a different way, they unconsciously followed God's law. In the Qur'an it says, 'They planned, and God planned, and God is the best of planners.'

The 'restoration of Israel' can be seen in the same way, passing from Zionist dream and pre-WWII taboo to idea whose time had, suddenly, come. However, just as the catalyst, the Shoah itself, had been extraordinary, so too would be the implications of the restoration. The Jews were surely not simply to be restored, as if exile had never been their portion, as if God had changed His mind, or felt sorry. Things had changed – the Jews had changed and the Holy Land had changed. The Nazis, agents and victims of history, acting on behalf of (they thought), or above, or without, God, had perpetrated, not a humbling, but the degradation of the Chosen People before they tried to destroy them and take their place and to, as Elie Wiesel says, 'kill God.' And they called Jews, strangely yet significantly, 'Musselmen', though the submission was hardly willing, and they were certainly not slaves to God. (Though in the deepest sense, they were, and we all are, slaves to God, which is what 'Israel' means in Arabic).

But where the survivors ended up there were Muslims, in Palestine, and this is why I believe all this is happening now. We are watching, buried beneath the nationalism, the secularism, the narrow religious understandings, the sheer pain and grief of history, the meeting of those who submit to God, Islam, in a position of weakness, with those who struggle with God, Israel, in a position of power (though this is not to be confused with 'wholly good/wholly bad'). But this is what it has all been leading to – Ishmael's 'great nation' and the other Arabian references in the Bible; the Messianic expectations among Jews at the times of both Jesus and Muhammad, and their rejection for bringing the 'wrong' message or being of the wrong origin; the expectation even of Shabbatai Zvi, the Jewish false Messiah of 1666, who became Muslim in the end; and then, finally, Israel. Some Jews called 1967 the Return to Repentance, though that has not happened yet. I believe Jews have been brought back to Israel to submit to God which, since the time of the Prophet Muhammad, has meant becoming Muslim.

In conclusion, for us as Muslims this clearly requires a different kind of struggle or *jihad*. Conventional struggle is unlikely to succeed, barring miracle, and the Palestinians, I'm sorry, don't seem pure enough for that. Currently, inasmuch as we are 'right', we are only right on a worldly level. As long as Israelis can continue to imply a claim to having God on their side they are likely to keep the US and much of the West on their side too, or at least not wholly on ours. More significantly, it is not going to change any hearts and to do that we are going to have to look deeply.

On a macro level, we are all going to have to give up something. It has long seemed to me that a genuine, religious resolution to this conflict is the only thing that will work and that it will involve Muslims, Christians and Jews being able to say, 'We were right (just not completely).' Christian veneration of Jesus will in some way be vindicated by his role in the Final Days, though he will be a Muslim. What we have is the Chosen Faith of Allah, and that is plenty. What we are not is a Chosen People. That role lies with the Jews and they now have to answer the question, Chosen for what? What they decide, and when, will clearly affect, and be affected by, us, but it is ultimately between them and God. 'Your Lord may well show mercy to you, but if you revert to your evil behaviour, We shall revert to chastising you.'

On a micro, personal level, and to answer the questions posed at the beginning, I believe we should:

i. encourage non-violent opposition to Israeli oppression and occupation in Israel (a prospect the Israelis *really* fear) and think in terms of the Treaty of Hudaybiyah rather than the siege of Khaybar. This includes removing the excuse for harder hearts that every suicide bomb attack on Israeli civilians provides

ii. campaign, protest and petition for an Israeli withdrawal from the West Bank and Gaza Strip and boycott Israeli produce until it happens

iii. provide as much humanitarian and religious support as we can for Palestinians in Palestine and refugees outside;

iv. promote positive contact with Jews who live outside Israel, including anti-Zionist religious groups such as Neturei Karta, and condemn attacks on Jews. Blind anti-Semitism (in the anti-Jewish sense) outside Israel is unIslamic and is a racist act rather than a pro-Palestinian one. If anything, attacks on Jews serve to reinforce the Zionist dictum that Jews are only safe in Israel.

v. engage in positive *dawa* that focuses on the spiritual paradox that is the people Israel in the land of Israel – a (largely atheist) group that claims the only meaningful relationship of *anyone* with a universal God, expressed through *struggle* with that God and that contravenes the moral imperatives of its own covenant and,

vi. pray 'that Allah will grant love and friendship between you and those whom you now hold as enemies' (Qur'an 60:7) and that they *do* see the error of their arrogance this time as they failed to see it in the time of the Prophet and before.

If we do this then at least we will be engaged in a form of *jihad* that we can, insh'Allah, win. Allah helps no one who does not try to help themselves, and ultimately He guides whom He will.

'By Time through the ages, truly, man is in loss, except those who believe and do righteous deeds and recommend one another to the Truth and recommend one another to patience and constancy.' (103: 1-3)

CHECKPOINT HUWARA, NABLUS

What happens to a dream deferred?
Does it dry up like a raisin in the sun
Or fester like a sore
And then run
Does it stink like rotten meat?
Or crust over
Like a syrupy sweet?
Maybe it just sags like a heavy load.
Or does it explode?
(Langston Hughes)

Firstly the name. They don't really check anything. They ask some people to open bags but they don't look further than the top towel or pair of jeans. They don't scan cards. It's not about security. They just look at your ID card and maybe ask where you're going. But they let it take ages. Checkpoints are inefficient, unfair and unpleasant, and that seems to be the point.

For foreigners, they're also unpredictable. The first time I went through with my family two weeks ago, we walked down the middle of the road on the advice of waiting Palestinians. A soldier looked at us quizzically but did nothing. I saw a clip on TV just after of the same checkpoint and a demonstration. It was a bit noisy but nothing untoward until a soldier threw a tear gas grenade in. Then there was mayhem. But our coming out again after that was also easy.

The next time, we got separated. My wife and children went through in the women's line, which is faster, while I got stuck at the back of the non-moving men's queue until I decided to do the middle-of-the-road option with a foreigner who had a mobile phone – essential here. As we faced off with a particularly unhelpful soldier – No! Go over there! – I tried to call an Israeli liaison officer I was on my way to see to pick up a travel permit. The soldier pushed us back – 'You are like schoolchildren so I treat you like that! Get BACK!' – while I told him what I was doing but he seemed to ignore it: 'How does it feel?' he said. 'How does it feel?' And then suddenly we were let through. Perhaps he, or someone, did realise I was speaking to someone higher-ranking than him.

He referred to it as a 'favour' two days later when we had to go back through the same checkpoint but he was almost a mediator for his extremely aggressive immediate superior. These two, and a round-faced, rosy-cheeked soldier, who confused our five-year old by being friendly, were the only ones manning the Nablus-in checkpoint. When we arrived they were checking a car that was hoping to go to hospital, a boy screaming inside. There didn't seem to be too many people, women and parents were moving through and pushing in and after about 20 minutes we were called forward. We walked past a medic and two young Palestinian men, squatting on the ground, their hands bound with the typical plastic straps.

No! said the sergeant. Go back home! He then directs this just at me because my wife has Palestinian ID and her family live in Nablus. Why? No tourists! What if we go on? You will be arrested! Go back! I'm not going back. Wait here then. Then what? Then nothing. No tourists.

This all takes place in very raised voices and our five-year old is screaming at us to go back and pleading with the soldiers not to kill us. The sergeant tries to assure her that they're not going to kill anybody. Perhaps they really believe this but nights in Balata refugee camp across the road from where we're staying have been filled with the sounds of someone at least trying.

All this time no-one else has come through. The round-faced soldier is left on his own while the sergeant and the would-be school-teacher go off and search some donkey carts, whose donkeys then escape. People suspect a relatively soft touch and try to edge up. They are sent back. He says he is not allowed to let anyone through. It is midday and very hot.

The soldier talks to my daughter, says she is a nice girl and has a nice name. He'd let us through if he were in charge but the sergeant, whose parents were injured in a suicide bombing this year he says, is boss today. He talks about terrorists. He points to the medic who had tried to bring a pair of binoculars through. They use them to spy on us, he says, and then a terrorist will come and blow himself up here.

While this is going on, the two hand-tied youths are becoming less so. Passers-by obscure them from the not very interested soldier, but they don't try and rush him. They hadn't, by all accounts, done anything and they don't try to do anything now. The soldier gives a young boy who has been hanging around some water to give them. My mother-in-law says these boys are informers, a fairly well-hidden human rights abuse this, and that prisoners like these are the ones who make up the numbers in the 'goodwill gesture' prisoner releases that occur when the peace process gets its kick starts.

I manage to borrow a mobile phone and ask the British Consulate if they can do anything. They say they will try but that I will need a phone. The one that I borrowed belongs to a man back 'behind the plastic', watching with the other men, and waiting. At one point, their anger erupts and there is a fight within the group. I'm reminded of the cynical old badge slogan, 'Help the police, beat yourself up'.

Back from the donkeys, the rough sergeant thinks it's all getting out of hand and shouts over the tannoy that the checkpoint is closed. He messes about with the radio, playing some jolly muzak to us very loud, then laughs and tuts and clucks into the mike. There is a fine line between enjoying the arrogance of your position and being fearful and nervous. He walks it. A jeering jeep going past is just arrogant.

After a while he gets bored with this and just watches our 1½ year-old as she chases round the feet of the people coming through the other way. I wonder, but have no way of knowing, whether he reflects on anything as he does so.

By now, a few families are being allowed through. The man who lent me the mobile tries his luck again, hoping that his helpfulness might count for something. He is turned back again and snatches the phone back from me. When the Consulate next rings they get an earful from him. It was the British who started all this after all.

A school teacher tests the plastic ties on one of the youths. The Palestinian strips them off his wrists with ease. The soldier tries to look unimpressed. Are you happy now? he says. Happier than you, the Palestinian replies. This generally seems to be true. The soldier walks off, looking puzzledly at the plastic and testing it.

Then two Americans from the International Solidarity Movement arrive, heading for Nablus. They are not allowed through and they ask about the two bound men and say they want to record and film them. Then suddenly another man appears. He is very tall, very strong and he wants to get through. He is desperate, not like the other mainly older men who have overstepped the mark. The two rougher soldiers shift into action, cocking their guns and shouting at him in Hebrew to sit and put his hands up. The man doesn't and curses the sergeant's mother. A new young soldier steps in to try to defuse the situation but is told to get out of it by the sergeant. It's hard to see how this can end in any way other than violence. I think they're going to shoot him. I am shocked to find that I feel angry with him for messing up our chances of getting in. Probably exactly, somewhere, what people are feeling about us.

The two Americans, one an Arabic speaker it seems, try to both calm the situation and confront the soldiers. The woman shouts at the sergeant, The man's father is dying, he's come all the way up from Bethlehem and you just say, No, go back. How do you think he feels? Put yourself in his shoes!

I'm using her phone while this is going on, and the Consulate tells me that the Israelis have said I can go through. They should be radioing the checkpoint. As we speak, the new soldier gets a message on the walkie-talkie which he relays to the sergeant who gestures us to go through. It took two hours.

It took two hours and we're British. We've got a Consulate and, as some would say, we've just fought a war for these people. While we're standing there, someone, somewhere is doing something on our behalf. People bother to speak to us, even if it's only to be rude, and they let us stand in the middle, not ignored, out of sight, out of mind. God willing, we're leaving in four days. This is not every day for us. But for the rest of the day I feel the opposite of the patience and understanding I felt at the checkpoint. I feel a grievance against everyone immediately around me, as if they, representatives of the world, owe me something. As a naïve incomer and soon to be leaver I feel I can process this in some way, make sense of it and have a glimpse of how much humanity gets lost in the grand meta-narrative that this is part of. But I am also awful to be with.

It was small. No-one died there. (Though the man's father did, I found out next day). Maybe even some small change happened for some, because of the ISM people or even because of our children. But we were only there for two hours. Men were waiting before we arrived and were waiting when we left. My mother-in-law, over 60, waited five hours earlier in the week to go and see her husband in Ramallah where he'd been taken after a heart attack. And this is normal. This is every day. This is post-unveiling of the roadmap. And people wonder why the Palestinians don't trust the Israelis' intentions and why they keep rejecting peace.

I hate the violence. I deplore the attacks on civilians on both sides and I believe that suicide bombing is immoral and unIslamic, and that any ends it achieves will be marred by the means. But humiliation at checkpoints is one of the reasons given by bright, well-adjusted young people who strap on nail bombs and explosives and go into Jerusalem. From my mere two hours there, once, I can glimpse how they got to go down that road. For perhaps just one second, the Israelis will have to see them after looking past them for so long. They will be eating in a restaurant and suddenly, there's a commotion, a dark figure, shouting, light, sound, pain, and death.

A CHINK OF LIGHT

The hole in the wall story was one of many, and many of those were brutal, but it stayed with me because there have often been stories like this in Palestine. It would be easier if it were not there, easier if this were, say, Chechnya, where there seem to be few such 'niceties'. But in Abu Dis, just outside Jerusalem, a Palestinian family are fighting it out in the courts with the Israelis to have the hole in the wall next to their house left open. It seems like a pretty ineffective totalitarian state if they can't just build a wall where they want; it's hardly been a problem elsewhere.

In the photo you can see it, a small break in the solid band of grey. A chink of light. The hole is used to link families and to transport bodies for burial in the cemetery and it imposes arbitrary access and hours-long journeys that used to take minutes, so is typical of the oppression that the 'Security Wall' brings. Yet it also symbolises, and let's not make too much of this, and as the speaker says, it will probably be closed soon, but it also symbolises a word that I haven't used (as paragraph two ends) yet. Hope. Some hope in Palestine does come from the Israelis themselves.

For a People of the Book, it is not so surprising that the Jews have produced many lawyers. Moses was the law bringer who cried justice for his people thousands of years ago. Jesus, we understand, was sent to a people who were mainly concerned with the letter of the law rather than its spirit. These days, there are the legendary pigs-on-stilts ('No swine shall be bred on the Land of Israel'), and a complicated bit of Aramaic legalese on the wall of Israeli banks exempts all parties from the ban on interest-taking and some lawyers do this and some do that. There have been several notable Jewish Israeli human rights lawyers who have fought for the Palestinians. So there it is. Hope. Passing stories, but a continuing stream of them.

Another. The speaker spoke of her confrontation with one particular, and particularly angry, soldier. He was furious with her and with the Palestinians, but she kept her head and eventually said that she felt sorry for him. Yes, he said, and he told her that 'they' were crazy. 'They', the settlers who lived in Hebron's centre, would actually beat him up. One had even reported him for some sex act with another soldier in a watchtower. The soldier said it was a lie but no-one official ever asked him – they simply took the settler's word. The result was an unbroken 46-day stretch of duty. As the speaker said, we shouldn't be surprised at the excesses these soldiers sometimes commit. Like so many on both sides, they are under enormous pressure and in a state of fear, a state which can hardly produce peace.

Like many people you meet in Palestine, the speaker seems to typify a condition whereby this pressure actually touches the point of greatest meaning in the self. (I also suspect that for some, over time, it distorts it). However, unlike the Palestinians and the Israeli soldiers, her position, and that of other outsiders, including the settlers (and myself), is chosen. It's therefore a bit of a dubious one in terms of sanity. I mentioned that I had once overheard a conversation between two prospective American settlers who were hoping to move to Qiryat Arba, the Jewish settlement just outside Hebron. One said that you have to pass psychological tests to live there. Someone from the audience quipped that the ones who failed got to live *inside* the city. There, they live cheek by buffer zone by jowl with the Palestinian Hebronites who have to have wire mesh pinned over their narrow streets because of the settlers' hobby of pinging boulders onto their heads.

Yet even in understanding this, the wellsprings of this position, there is hope. As Muslims, we are expected, required, to be optimistic, to believe that Allah has willed all this as so. Earlier in the day, the hadith in which the Prophet, peace be upon him, says thrice, Do not be angry, was linked to our responses to suicide bombing. Perhaps by feeling and understanding, rather than simply forbidding, our own anger, we can transcend it and then not project it on to others. Anger is, as was said, often an expression of anger at the self: 'Allah will not change our condition unless we change our selves.'

A closing talk on the day was not explicitly on Palestine, but in speaking of the Verse of Light with its mention of olive oil and neither east nor west, why not? The speaker spoke, not of the difficulty of these times, but the opportunity we have to bring light into the darkness.

Allah is the Light of the heavens and the earth. The parable of His Light is as if it were a niche and within it a lamp. The lamp is enclosed in glass, the glass as it were a brilliant star, lit from a blessed tree, an olive, neither of the East nor of the West, whose oil is well-nigh luminous, though the fire scarce touched it. Light upon Light! Allah guides to His Light whom He wills: Allah doth set forth parables for men, and Allah doth know all things.' (24:35-6)

Another speaker, speaking of the keys to successful fasting, said that because he was from Manchester, he didn't need to shout. All this put me in mind of another Mancunian who once sang, in tones of plaintive fatalism, 'There is a light that never goes out' on an album that could well have been 'Louder than Bombs'.[10]

[10] Actually, it's on 'The World Won't Listen' and was originally on 'The Queen is Dead'; pessimistic, and geographically irrelevant respectively.

INESCAPABLE REALITIES

Unlike Gaza, the West Bank lives a split reality with fault lines between here and there, now and then, day and night. The Old City of Nablus I'd imagined would be devastated, but it has been mostly rebuilt, the Church of the Nativity in Bethlehem shows little sign of the siege earlier in the year and was host to simultaneous christening, wedding and funeral while we were there. They could make a film about it! And elsewhere too, life goes on. The markets are busy, flowers still grow, mothers continue to give birth, my new nephew Muhammad, for example. Somehow this surprises.

But usually elsewhere, houses are demolished and orchards uprooted. The prison in Nablus is a shell, the epicentre of the attack a portrait of Yasser Arafat that used to cover the wall. His headquarters in Ramallah is nearly flattened. At the other end of the creative process, the newly-built wall supposedly protecting Israel from suicide bombers, cuts chunks into the West Bank, cuts off water sources and access to fields. Travelling between towns, there are checkpoints when you leave one and arrive at another, checkpoints you have to pass through on foot, making every journey a minimum of three taxis or buses and the waits in between grinding, frustrating experiences that depend on previously hard-won travel permits. This is where occupation hits most – on roads and on maps.

At night, tanks recorrugate the road outside my flat that separates town from refugee camp. Machine-gun fire rips through the night. Flares light up the sky at dawn prayer. Many Palestinians don't flinch or wake up. This is still better than a few months ago when the residents of Nablus were confined to their homes for over a hundred days of the year.

Since the beginning of June there's been a split between up and down, and in and out. 'Up' in Israel, many were amazed and/or outraged that Sharon used the Hebrew word '*kibbush*' – occupation – five times in a speech, saying it hurt Israelis and Palestinians. A peacenik spokesman said it released a new dynamic, a settler that it went against the ideological foundation of the Likud party. So much of the problem in Israel was a 'conflict of languages.' A paper headlined 'Sharon Akshav', punning on the name of Peace Now, Shalom Akshav. Downstairs, the conflict was less semantic.

With the Aqaba summit, words of optimism and peace are heard in the media while on the ground, nothing seems to change. Children throw stones at an army bulldozer that has been blocking off a road in Nablus so it comes back and seals off their access on to the main road. There is still firing at night, even before the soldiers are killed in Gaza. According to a writer in Al Quds, the Palestinian Arabic daily paper, the Israelis have 14 reservations to the Road Map, which doesn't even promise anything about Jerusalem or refugees. These 14 would destroy any hopes of peace if respected.

Then, of course, the realities merge, with the soldiers killed in Gaza, then the attempted assassination of Hamas spokesman, Rantizi, the suicide bombing in Jerusalem, further assassinations in Gaza, again with loss of civilian life, and further clashes throughout the West Bank.

Through all this, and in quieter moments, people try to make sense of what is happening with theoretical constructs. A common Muslim position is that the Israeli Jews of today are no relation to the Children of Israel talked about in the Qur'an but descendants of a Crimean tribe, the Khazars, who converted en masse in obedience to their king. They are effectively interlopers, runs the argument, and so should leave.

A similar relativistic argument has long run in the world of archaeology. Here, revisionists argue that the traditional focus of local archaeology on the Biblical has meant that huge spans of effectively ethnic Palestinian time have been ignored in order to focus on the minority periods of Jewish presence or ascendancy. This serves as a motif for the grossly unfair way the political priorities are weighed up in current Middle East discourse.

I met the same thing again in discussion with the editor of Palestinian English language weekly, the Jerusalem Times. He dismissed the idea of the Jews as Chosen People as being an irrelevant myth. They were simply another group, like the Armenians or Greeks, who happened to be powerful and who were taking Palestinian land. (And so didn't want any article I should write on that subject. Me bitter?).

A lot of the young simply choose the lifestyle option. Smoke, flirt through checkpoints if female, date, hope it ignores me.

The thread that runs through these is the desire to wish reality into the shape of something that fits a world-view. On the Israeli side, as well as this literally describing the way the wall is seen, tortuous debates go on as to whether the territories are occupied 'in the classic definition of international law.' If they are not, runs one side of the argument, then Israel is not legally obliged to refrain from building settlements. Just change the law and the problem will be gone. Other realists shun such legal niceties. Remove the Palestinians and the problem will be gone. You couldn't make this stuff up!

I know lots of people say otherwise, but I think they're wrong. I believe that beneath all this, the reality is that this is, at least de facto, a religious conflict. A critical mass of people, in one way or another, see the meaning and outcome as being connected to God. The religiously-inspired settlers believe they are following this 'transcendental imperative' in opposing any compromise with non-believers. They hope that through their marriage of convenience with the ruling Likud party, non-fundamentalists will have such a vested interest in the relationship that they will become whole-hearted converts. This, in its turn, will transform Israeli society and drag a reluctant world towards redemption. In America particularly, fundamentalist Christians go along with this to the point of believing that all this will bring about a Jesus-led Christian redemption of the world.

In the mosques, meanwhile, the Friday sermon talks about the relationship between the Prophet Muhammad, peace be upon him, and the Jews in Madina. There, the Prophet asked the Jews to embrace Islam and achieve security. Someone had been expected by them but the Prophet Muhammad was rejected because he was not a Jew, and he told those early Muslims that the Day of Judgement would not come until huge groups fought against each other. The claim being the same; God is on their side.

And, though we might wish otherwise, here we are. At the end of the day, the fundamental religious Jewish position is that there will be peace when Israel is on at least one bank of the Jordan. Non-Jews will be allowed to leave or convert. The fundamental Christian position, one of the reasons for support for the Jewish State, is that the Jews, gathered in the land of his birth, will accept Jesus as Saviour and Messiah. The fundamental Muslim position is that the solution is Islam and these are Muslim lands. I have no problem with that, but because of my own experience, do not see any personally held religious position as fixed in stone.

What I do see it as, is as a question of our relationship with God. That's what I came here looking for an answer to. And it changed me. In the end it was put to me very simply. Struggle or submit. God knows the ego hates to do the latter but I believe that that is the choice, the destiny, we all face. And that we will face even clearer soon, starting here in Israel, in Palestine. The Holy Land. And there is hope.

I had a dream….

Actually, I've had at least two.

II. THE UNCROWNED QUEEN – Nablus (2005-7)

NABLUS - THE UNCROWNED QUEEN

Why the uncrowned Queen? Cynics would say it is something to do with the ring of jewels around the town that you can see at night, the distinctive yellow lights of settlements. It could be a reference to what is called the bracelet of Kabla, whose symbols tell the mythical story of the virgin of Nablus, and which was stolen by the Israelis, one of many archaeological artefacts not currently with us. It could be my wife, who is from here! I'd like to think that it is a reference to the future potential of this place, my home for the last year and a half, but I think it is something to do with the crusaders.

In the period that culminated in Salah al-Din's invasion in 1187, there was a succession crisis for the crusaders. When Baldwin V died in 1186, one of the claimants, Isabella, and regent elect, Raymond of Tripoli, took his body to Tiberias for burial. Meanwhile, Sybilla, Baldwin's sister, and her unpopular husband, Guy de Lusignan, had themselves crowned in the Church of the Holy Sepulchre in Jerusalem. Isabella and her husband Humphrey of Tibnine gathered in Nablus, planning to have themselves crowned there, but, at the last moment, Humphrey fled and submitted to Sybilla and Guy, ending the rebellion. Isabella remained the uncrowned queen, so that fits, though I think they all add to that rather romantic, mysterious name.

Romance isn't a usual association with Nablus but I've always had pleasant associations with the city. The journey to Nablus from Jerusalem in a *servees* taxi used to be one of the most beautiful journeys I knew here, or anywhere. It was a bit slow but to travel just before sunset was exquisite, with the rocky hills, olive groves and winding road. It's much more direct now but, because of checkpoints, often much slower. The big one at Huwara is not usually a problem when going into Nablus, but coming out it usually causes long delays, assuming you have even got the right papers. Because of this, it now literally defines Nablus, the biggest city on the West Bank; many people simply do not go out of the confines of the city and haven't done so since the beginning of the second Intifada.

If its position between two mountains had made it a trifle cut off in the past, this enclosure has given Nablus something of a reputation, not entirely unlike that of Gaza, as a place you can't or shouldn't go to, a reputation that doesn't do the place justice. The particularity of the city and its inhabitants owes much to its position and to its history and the interplay of the two so, beginning after Huwara, we will follow a route through the city that will give at least a taste of this, and suggest that, even if not this week, Nablus is a place worth going to.

After Huwara you take a left and follow the road into town, more or less round the base of Mount Gerizim. On your right you can see Balata refugee camp, home to thousands of families who define themselves as coming from Jaffa and central Palestine rather than Nablus. It is one of the most militant in the West Bank and Israeli jeeps and armoured cars come up the same road with Balata as their destination. Many nights and early mornings are punctuated by their gunfire, though more recently, there has also been inter-factional fighting.

Within a stone's throw (the standard yardstick for measuring distance among writers in the Holy Land) of this modern bastion of resistance are three sites of Biblical and historic interest, reminders that Nablus has deep roots, a history of conflict, and potential as a big tourist draw in better times. (There are over 80 such sites here). Just to the right of the road at the junction you can see a brown dome among three green ones, topped with a cross rather than a crescent. It is the recently restored church that houses Jacob's Well, bought by the ancient patriarch according to the Bible, and the place where Jesus drank water given to him by a Samaritan woman who accepted him as Messiah, an act that for Christians symbolises Jesus' breaking the narrow confines of Judaism to embrace the whole tribe of Israel.

Down the dip from the junction is, according to the Bible, the tomb of Jacob's favourite son, Joseph. It has been a mosque but from 1967 to 2000, as well as being a military camp, it was a Jewish shrine and place of study; being the third holiest place in Judaism. Having a military base with settlers almost inside a refugee camp was asking for trouble and in October 2000, clashes broke out around the tomb in which six Palestinians and one Israeli were killed. When the Israelis finally pulled out, the tomb was destroyed, at least partly to stop them returning. It remains a shell and a sad precedent.

Almost behind it is the ruin of the ancient city of Balata, the original Shekhem. It has Biblical connections to Abraham and Joshua, among others, and some remarkably well preserved walls and gatehouses, ancient bastions of resistance. For all these reasons, it has the potential to be Nablus' premier archaeological site.

The route into town next passes the massive prison on the left. Built by the Turks, it served the British, the Israelis and the Palestinians before it was devastated by the Israelis in 2006. Gone is the massive painted picture of Yasser Arafat that used to adorn the walls. Gone are the walls. Instead, the iron skeleton of the building hangs with pieces of concrete still attached, giving it an odd appearance of melting. I'd once fancied this as a museum of some sort, but can't see that now.

When you get to the centre of town, between the hospital and the vegetable market you can see a stone milepost, which directs you to Sabastia, the Samaria of the Bible and the capital of then Israel, as opposed to Judea, and home to some impressive remains. Then, just behind the vegetable sellers, there is a deep drop, at the bottom of which is a very impressive, though neglected, Roman amphitheatre. If you had taken the turning just after the ex-prison and followed that road along some 400 meters you would have found the other major Roman remain here, another amphitheatre, tucked into someone's back yard. It is this that is featured on the mosaic map at Madaba in Jordan and its size (it was the largest in the Middle East and had a capacity of over 6000 people) is the reason that archaeologists have surmised that Flavia Neapolis, as the Roman general Vespasian named the new town in 72 CE, was correspondingly large.

Passing through the vegetable market you come to the *Dawar*, venue for quite frequent political rallies, and beyond it, the old city. This is home to a *souq* that rivals Jerusalem's in its atmosphere and, more than any other place, defines the atmosphere and the identity of the town as Arab and predominantly Muslim, and banishes the idea that nothing interesting or beautiful has happened here in the last 2000 years. As well as all the food and other goods you might need, there is a Turkish bath that was built around 1840, the Tujar Khan, the Manara clock tower, the Old Sayara Square, the Great Mosque (Jame' al-Kabir), one of over 30 mosques in the city, and the attractive Yasmeena Hotel. Many of these date from the Ottoman era and are some of the few buildings that survived the massive 1927 earthquake. The old city is unfortunately a frequent target for Israeli raids, including the massive siege of 2002 that left so much damage, though, like the people who live here, it seems to have a tremendous capacity to survive this kind of treatment.

From the old city, you can go up the hill past the library, home of a very impressive English section (and Arabic) and a discarded Napoleonic cannon. Straight up would take you to the university and beyond to the new site, beyond which the land suddenly falls away to reveal a hilly landscape that stretches to the coast. Alternatively, the even more interesting route is to turn left just before the cemetery and follow the road up Mount Gerizim, the Biblically-named blessed mountain, twin of Ebal, the cursed one, across the valley. These two mountains define the elongated shape of Nablus and, if conversations do indeed echo off them, the sometimes gossipy nature of Nabulsi social life.

At the top of Gerizim is a village that is home to the Samaritans, with the tribe of Judah, one of the two surviving twelve tribes. There are some 700 of them, making them the smallest religious minority in the world, and they have clung on to their life on what they believe is the site of both Abraham's would-be sacrifice and the Temple. You can still see the place where they believe the sacrifice took place; and ruins left by the Greeks, Romans, Byzantines and Salah e-Din; a fantastic panoramic view, and, oh, the Israeli observation post that has been watching you since you came into town.

That, and much more, is Nablus. Unfortunately, the situation hardly encourages prioritising the care of all these historic sites and it can sometimes cause a certain wariness of strangers. However, I've lived here for nearly one and a half interesting years and as long as I don't wear a bicycle helmet, I find people friendly, helpful and often ironically humorous about 'the situation.' Jenin may have its murals; Ramallah, its share of the culture (though a lot more classical music makes its way up here than you'd expect); Bethlehem, the infrastructure to cope with tourists and the Christian sites to show them, if they come; and Hebron, the Ibrahimi Mosque, grapes and good jokes, but Nablus has a distinctive identity all of its own and a huge amount to offer visitors. And, yes, that includes the kannafa.

ANGELS WORKING OVERTIME[11]

Someone, somewhere has decided that what a place like Nablus in particular, and the West Bank in general, needs is some Mozart, some classical music to civilise our turbulent state, our troubled souls. As I sit here and listen to it I don't know what it is that moves me most. Is it the dissonance or the resonance? Is it how out of place the music almost seems, so European, 'cultured', 'refined'? Or is it that it echoes something universal; that the music of arguably the greatest composer ever is ultimately not about masked balls and soirees but about the human spirit? The trick, it seems, is to make my head shut up and listen.

Five musicians begin, two violins, viola, cello, visiting British musicians with the Choir of London, and on clarinet, regular visitor Douglas Metcalf, based in Ramallah. The string instruments weave a textured fabric of sound that is immensely full for so few, and the clarinet adds the soothing sound of human breath. Many of the pieces are very spiritual in their tone and I think of angels working overtime here. Somehow my head, that still won't entirely be quiet, tries to picture what I am hearing, so I can then describe it in words, as if that is somehow the point. I wonder if music before Mozart, Bach et al, was pure spirit, and after, Beethoven et al, pictorial and emotional, and Mozart described the spirit coming down to earth. Somehow. The instruments interplay themes and melodies with grace and feeling and all I see are clouds and blue sky and a feeling of the human spirit and the clarinettist semi-conducting the musicians with his head and eyes. And then the choir come out and sing one gloriously tender song with the musicians and go off again and hot little tears are rolling down my cheeks.

After the break, which coincides with the *adhan*, the call to prayer, appropriately enough, the choir sing more. Speaking to them in the break and after, they are normal Brits, but put them together and they can both soothe and sing pure surges of spiritual joy. In the *Miserere*, they perform a call and response of soloist/choir, with the soloist moving around the balcony, 'up in the gods' as theatre-speak has it.

---

[11] Palestine Mozart Festival: Chamber & Choral Classics with the Choir of London at the Zafer Al-Masri Foundation, Nablus, Thursday 5 April 2007

When they finish, the audience sits there wondering if that's it. The question in the air is, I suppose, do we now just go back to reality, or have we just met a deeper one?

LA MACHINE[12]

It's a good time to be reminded that football is not the only universal language, and I'm not talking about English or computers either, though the name of the main group here, La Machine, might make you think so. Music has been around a lot longer, and, despite the name, the music of La Machine is very human.

It's to the credit of the French Cultural Centre that they've gone ahead in reminding us of that in these difficult times by organising a week-long music festival that brings French music to all parts of Palestine. If it's anything as good as that of La Machine, it is not out of place here.

The evening was a nice blend of East and West, beginning with the Palestinian police brass band, followed by some excellent Dabka from the children of Askar Camp's Masha'al Falasteen and various performances from young musicians from the Nablus Children's Cultural Centre. Lucky them to be followed by the pulsing heights of French turbo-folk.

The Machine of their name presumably refers to a strange instrument, something between a guitar and a wind-up music box, that is central to La Machine's distinctive sound and sounds nothing much like either. The round and round sound carries the rhythm and melody and over this the others play pulsing double bass, percussion and the leader plays bagpipes, violin, sings and even dances. The whole is an organic stew of various tastes that are, at the same time, very central French mountain, but also echo anything between the Maghrib and Afghanistan, Scotland and the Sudan.

They play in Hebron on 22 June and Gaza on 25 June and there are other events in all the six main Palestinian towns. Bienvenue a La Machine et Merci.

---

[12] 17 June 2006, Childhood Happiness Centre, Nablus

INTERNATIONAL BAD DRIVING WEEK COMES TO TOWN

Breakneck acceleration. Car horns hoot at all times. Brakes screech. Cars drive the wrong way down streets. Traffic lights change irrelevantly. Yes, without the benefit of any advance publicity, the ever-popular International Bad Driving Week is being celebrated enthusiastically with events all across town.

'People are really excited and we've been amazed at the response,' says a spokesperson for the event, which is becoming a regular feature of the driver's year all across the West Bank. 'Everyone seems to be contributing in some way, even pedestrians.'

I speak to a driver who's stopped for a coffee at some traffic lights, appropriately enough, outside the hospital. 'People are quite stubborn here,' he says, as cars drive past through a red light, nearly hitting a couple of people standing in the road talking. 'What drivers need to understand is that the colours of the traffic lights are just there to make the town look nice. Like car indicating lights. Green means Go is Good! That's easy to remember, lots of 'G's, but if people really start to think that Red means Stop I can't think where it will end. For a start, the tomato industry will collapse!'

He then starts to talk like he could talk all day about the yellow light being like the sun ripening the tomatoes from great height and the way the flashing indicators are like the stars at night and cars behind him hoot their horns like they want a fight and, as the green light turns red, he pulls away.

At the town's Driving Academy an instructor explains one of the problems of trying to encourage bad driving: 'People have a natural instinct when they pull out into moving traffic to look behind them to make sure that they're not going to be hit by a car from the side or behind. We try to unteach this.' He shows me a complicated brace-like contraption that prevents drivers turning their heads. It includes a black patch to block off the side mirror.

'We do a crash course here that's really effective. After a while, not looking just becomes second nature, as you can see from the way people drive. If you're really stuck, just break off your side mirror and go,' he says. 'If something's coming, it's not your problem.'

At the university's Centre for Research into Automobile and Street Hospitalisation (CRASH!), a psychologist explains this idea further. 'People are usually very resistant to the idea of being bad drivers. It's always the other person's fault. In fact, we've done a lot of research where we've interviewed people after accidents and there is a long chain of people who someone thinks is responsible, but each person in the chain says it's not them. In the end we've found there is just one person responsible for all the crashes. It's logical really.'

I ask if this is really true; one person is responsible for all the traffic problems in town? 'That's right. They live near the university, but I can't say who it is,' says the slightly blushing psychologist, who lives near the university, incidentally.

'That's why this week is so good for people. We can be proud of something that we can all take ownership of together. We're bad drivers and we're proud. We don't need the Israelis to kill us. We can do it ourselves!'

I see this pride on the face of the taxi driver when he laughs as I try to put on my safety belt. As I go home I pass the children walking home down the road from school carrying banners proclaiming: 'Use the sidewalk for what it is for! Ummm… not quite sure exactly…' I smile as I see a car parked in such a way that I don't even know which side of the road it's supposed to be parked on. And I whoop for joy as a dense cloud of exhaust smoke swallows up the car that has just dropped me off. Bad Driving Week? I think this could run and run!

LIKE PEACE NEEDS A BICYCLE…

'Asira Shamilya is 5kms to the north of Nablus and situated behind Mount Ebal, the highest mountain in the West Bank. Like most Palestinian villages, probably, it does not appear to have much that is distinctive about it at first. It is long established but mostly fairly recently-built. It is set amid the hills and olive trees and the air is good but it's not too remote to be immune from occupation. Sound familiar? However, it does have a bit of a reputation and it's a good one, and I had a nice day there. My wife, who is from Nablus, used to come here for picnics and it's still a pleasant place to cycle round, with its intense midday heat blanket, dusty pine smells, birdcalls and bees and, apart from that, an incredible silence. It has also dealt in a way that may not be spectacular, but that seems to be effective, with some of the pressures of occupation.

We cycled to an example of one of these, a school that is built 7 kms from the village, serving the teenage boys of 'Asira and nearby villages. Not an obvious location unless you have it explained that some settlers and the Israeli army had once eyed it up as a nice little place in the country and had made moves to build the dream. This prompted locals to do a big fund-raise to get a school built there instead, before it got to be declared a military zone or uncultivated land or some such legal nicety. The villagers built their school and for their pains it became a constant site of conflict in the first years of the second intifada. A sniper shot one student trying to get back to his village – a memorial marks the place - and at one stage soldiers closed the school and actually used it as a holding area for prisoners. Nice to think you're being taught in a room where your father or brother had been held prisoner, or worse. At other times, gas was thrown into the school and soldiers would often taunt students going in and coming out. What is interesting, and I don't know how much this is an 'Asira thing, though it had already come up in a different context, is that the students were instructed not to respond. Don't rise to the bait. Don't throw stones. And they won. It's a small victory, but the school is still there, still working. It reminds me of what a student of mine once said, on the subject of litter: we should tackle the problem as if the occupation isn't there. 'Asira, perhaps, tries to tackle the problem of the occupation as if it's not there. Not always easy.

My guide for the day I had first met in Nablus a month before. He was going to spot me easily. On a bike, over 40 and foreign, but he didn't say what he'd look like. But there he was, by the side of the main street going into Nablus, sporting what I can only call a handlebar moustache.

First thing he had to do was buy some flowers for his garden. He's unusual; he looks Prussian and he likes to grow sweet peas - 'the mouth of the fish' he tells me - when he's bussed them back to his village on the back of his bike. But those aren't the only ways (nor the fact that he keeps cats). He has a few stories to tell.

We go upstairs to his office in the Refugee Affairs Department, past his rather nice-looking mountain bike, very cool but for the green plastic basket on the back, the practical bit for, among other things, sweet peas. Then he sits framed next to the window overlooking the hills around the town and he tells me about a women's cyclist group that are arriving today and how they're probably going to be whisked off to Jerusalem and maybe Ramallah and Bethlehem.

'We're the only bike group in the West Bank, but no-one wants to come up to the north of the West Bank because it's too difficult. Too many checkpoints. But that's the whole point.'

He tells me that he started cycling in 3½ years ago because it took too long to get into town. I cycled in one day, 10 kilometres around the mountains and I rang the people who I'd left in the queue and they were still there.

A bike is a funny thing here. Neither fish nor fowl. It's not a car so you don't need a permit for it and you're not a pedestrian so you don't have to queue. You can just cycle up and go through if the soldiers are in a good mood. If…

He's had three bikes broken by soldiers who've found the conundrum his bike poses too difficult. 'They shot my wheels once and I had to get a taxi with the bike back to the village. I came back the next day and they sent me back, saying I needed a permit.'

Another time they held me for five hours in front of the people waiting at the checkpoint, and then they took me to Shavei Shimron, the settlement nearby. One of the soldiers put a rock on me and, the most disgusting thing, pissed on me.

He also describes the worst time, perhaps of his life, when he was stopped in the winter of 2000 on the way back from Nablus, where he'd bought winter clothes. He was stopped for hours, stripped, beaten and threatened with a troop-carrier to the head, until a message came on the radio telling the soldiers to leave the area.

'The vehicle left but what were they going to do with me? Kill me? One soldier came up behind me and kicked me down the hill. Then they left.

'I was right next to the village so people knew what was going on, but they hadn't been able to come out. Now they came with blankets and took me home. Both my arms were broken. I tell you, I watched our house being destroyed in '76 and I've seen plenty, but I'd never had anything like this.

'For me, I hate those soldiers. I asked them how they would feel if they were in my place and I in theirs, and they didn't answer. They just said, It will never happen.

'Afterwards, though, I felt stronger. When I was better, I went back to Nablus the same way, bought the same things from the same shop and came home the same way, passing the place where they'd tortured me. They'd told me it was a military zone, but it wasn't. Since then, it's given me power and strength.'

This empowerment has informed his life since, a lot of it with his bike. Generally, biking works, and he cycles to Nablus by bike every day. 'You can go over the mounds of earth that block roads and you can carry a bike through trees. But I don't care if I meet soldiers now. I prefer to, to talk with them.'

This attitude has got people in the village interested and now there are 25 cyclists, though only 10 bikes. 'The economic situation. We are trying to get more.' The group has had some donations, though requests to Israeli cycle groups have met with no response so far.

My guide described what villagers had tried to do themselves: 'With the closures, we started doing more things in the village, getting kids interested in cycling locally. Then last year we started to work with people who couldn't get to their land. 'Asira has olive trees that are hundreds of years old and it produces the best olive oil in the West Bank. But the army declared a lot of the olive trees to be in Military Zones and the village wanted to challenge this. The harvest is in November so we spent the month before preparing people. 'Whatever happens, just carry on. Don't react but don't stop working,' people were told.

So everyone went out to the trees during the olive harvest season. The old women prepared food, the children played in the trees and everyone else picked.

People got there at 6 and then at 8.30 the soldiers came and told everyone over loudspeakers to go home. Everyone just carried on although the soldiers fired in the air. In the end they came down, which was what we wanted, so we could speak to them. The officer told us all to leave. We asked him to look at what was happening. People working, old women singing traditional songs, kids playing. The officer told us to finish what we were doing that day and not come back.

The next day the villagers came back and carried on. The soldiers came back and the officer asked why they'd come back when they'd been told not to. Because it's our land and we're not doing any harm and we need to harvest the olives. Finish harvesting the olives and then don't come back, he told them.

When the harvesting was finished, we came back with experts to clean the trees, to cut back the dead branches and so on. When that was done, we came back with horses and donkeys to plough the land, and when we'd done that, we came back to rebuild the walls. And the soldiers just left us alone. Now the villagers can go to their land and other villages are interested.

So it can be done. Perhaps it needs *chutzpah*, as they say over there. Cheek. How to build small victories. The outcome is that 'Asira can at least harvest most of its olives, though this has created another problem that needs to be solved; the houses of the village are full of olives, olive oil and its products. It is very hard to export through Israel or even Jordan. As I said, it's not always easy.

As I leave, he gives me some still-warm *taboun* bread his wife had cooked and that we'd eaten for lunch. Oh, and two bars of fragrant, olive-oil soap. Slowly, slowly, 'Asira solves its olive surplus problems.

GANDHI AND ISLAM (OR, 'GANDHIAN ISLAM')

Is non-violence compatible with Islam?

Sometime between the two kidnappings of Israeli soldiers and the subsequent Israeli assaults on Gaza and Lebanon, the MBC2 TV channel screened the film 'Gandhi'. At some point in the film, someone speaks in favour of violent resistance and Gandhi, or Ben Kingsley anyway, says something like 'Maybe you are right, but it will not help you to achieve what you want.' It is a sentiment I often feel here in the West Bank. Though there is a significant tradition of non-violent resistance in Palestinian history, it has been steadily superseded in recent years by resistance of a violent kind as the only form worthy of attention. Israeli products are widely unboycotted in Palestinian stores, for example, while pictures of fighters who have been killed are everywhere. The struggle continues, but it is a minority that does it, it is necessarily secretive, it is justified by all because the Israelis do the same/worse and it provides the Israelis with reasons or excuses, depending on your viewpoint, for further violence. Maybe they are right, but I cannot see it helping them to achieve what is wanted, namely, an independent Palestine.

So where do I see Gandhi and his ideas fitting in with this? He led a movement that overturned massive odds and defeated the British Empire, and he did so in a way that at least left no hatred towards the opponent in India's non-violent revolution. In that, it succeeded, though he was unable to end conflict between Hindus and Muslims, nor to bring about the social revolution he had seen as necessary to achieving all of these aims.

There are many resonances between then and now, here and there: the massive odds, sectarian strife, and the need for some sort of social change. I would say that there is a tremendous need. The violence in Lebanon, Israel and the Occupied Territories can really lead nowhere, and an alternative is needed and, insh'Allah, wanted. It also has to be said that were any of these armed forces totally successful, they would bring in rulers that were, at least, highly authoritarian. Finally, there is the gentle thought that we are skirting round the edge of Armageddon here. If the conflict escalates, it will be catastrophic, and even if it doesn't, it has already cost millions in terms of weapons of war, and will cost millions to mend the damage those weapons have caused.

And it marginalises the ecological destruction that continues apace, here and elsewhere, warfare or no.

So, does Gandhi have something we Muslims can learn from? I believe that his message can be understood within the parameters of Muslim thought in two ways. Firstly, he was from a mixed area and his Hindu background was of the Pranami sect that combined Hindu and Muslim beliefs – no idols, and the Qur'an and the sacred books of the Vaishnavites were given equal honour. Secondly, if Islam is indeed a universal religion, it should not surprise us to find wisdom and truth in other traditions. This is not to say that everything Gandhi said or practised is consistent with or relevant to our beliefs as Muslims, as we will see later. However, if we look at common areas, it may allow us to see our position afresh.

One of the biggest of these was Gandhi's belief that political revolution and freedom had to come with social revolution. He spoke of the futility of mere religious knowledge and said, 'Every act has its spiritual, economic and social implications. The spirit is not separate.' He saw his role as religious and political leader in that light. This is an idea that is also at the heart of Islamic belief. Thus, he believed that India would only become truly free if it transformed itself and without that, independence would merely be the change of one power-seeking elite for another. He would even have accepted British rule had he felt that it allowed Indians to achieve these social/spiritual ends, though eventually he realised oppression was inseparable from the imperial system.

Related to this was Gandhi's understanding of the warfare of the Bhagavad-Gita as being a description of the struggle within the human heart, an idea very similar to the idea of the greater (internal) and lesser (external) *jihad* (struggle), and also to the concept of *ibada.*

In fact, Gandhi much admired the Prophet Muhammad, particularly his austerity. Neither enriched themselves through their political success. Gandhi went so far as to state that a higher standard of spiritual living required a lower level of material well-being and saw the key to all religions as being renunciation. There is a place for this in Islam, with *sawm*, fasting, being one of the five pillars, when discipline of our sensual selves is paramount as a means of spiritual purification. Patience is also a key concept. Gandhi said, 'Patient example is the only possible method to effect reform' and we can see this particularly in the example of the Prophet during the years of persecution in Makkah.

Both were also practical and compassionate men who saw the centrality of even the most basic aspects of human hygiene to a holistic spirituality. One writer described walking with Gandhi through the village near his *ashram* (model community) and seeing some men defecating in the open. Gandhi didn't shout at them, but with great pity and sorrow, buried their waste. I am reminded both of the hadith of the old Bedouin man who passed water in the mosque in the presence of the Prophet and his response – telling someone to douse the area with water – and also of the stories of pious imams discovered in the toilet areas of their mosques cleaning up after their congregations. Cleanliness in deed is next to godliness. In Gandhi's case, as with many of his beliefs-in-action, such an act achieved more than one function, being a stand both against untouchability and in favour of hygiene.

While one of the basic elements of his philosophy was simplified, spiritual communitarian living, the other was non-violent resistance, *satyagraha*, which means 'truth force'. It was from the former that the latter necessarily drew its strength. The point of it was a choice made by people who didn't fear to be violent, but chose to be non-violent and to fight using truth. In light of the mutual carnage that is being inflicted in the Middle East, regardless of whatever imbalances there may be, this is a significant point. He spoke of resistance without hostility with the aim of converting the opponent (who is an *opponent*, not an *enemy*) through suffering willingly endured. As another writer puts it in his biography of Gandhi, 'compromise with honour was implied in the whole conception, since the desired result was a settlement in which neither side would feel itself humiliated. In this way, both sides would in the end gain.' Wave your hands in the air and make a glorious noise if you can see that as a way out in Palestine, Lebanon, Iraq, India…!

This is not to say that there isn't a price (though people are paying highly already). The British met non-violent Indian protest with violence, including the massacre at Amritsar, where 379 people were killed by a totally unrepentant Brigadier-General Dyer. There is also no guarantee of success, though sometimes short-term failure or setbacks can lead to a new perspective. The above-mentioned massacre, for example, revealed the brute force that was inherent in British rule and effectively undermined any moral position.

Arguments, nonetheless, could be made against the appropriateness of Gandhian non-violence to our position. Demands were implicitly made on Gandhi's followers that were probably impossible to live up to; though married, Gandhi lived a chaste life for all of his later years as a means of preserving his energy. Similarly, his demands of simple living were also implicitly coercive if they were to be imposed on the nation as a whole. In a curious way, perhaps Gandhi recognised this and took on a heavier personal role. Thus, while in the earlier years of anti-British agitation, most of the actions taken were based on action by the masses, coordinated and supervised through trained non-violent activists, from 1932 onwards the greatest pressure brought to the campaign was Gandhi's fasts-unto-death. Such was Gandhiji's spiritual authority that the most violent were shamed into pacifism by the prospect of causing his death.

Something immensely powerful can nonetheless be taken from his story and example. Gandhi believed that non-violence was 'a strategy which, if only its practitioners were trained in self-restraint and as willing as soldiers to die for their cause, was infinitely flexible and could be used under any conditions and against any enemy.' He didn't, however, presume to be able to lead or advise other people's struggles, claiming 'I must make good here (India) first,' which leaves the understanding and interpreting of the different nuances of different struggles to those who are involved in them.

Some features, however, seem to be essential. In society-strengthening, education that teaches children to construct things with their hands instils creativity (Palestinian streets are full of the sounds of bottles breaking, in symbolic resistance to Israeli armoured car tyres or just out of frustration) and keeps alive a handicraft tradition that can be a source of income and an alternative to imported plastic commodities. This, and actions like boycotts, are part of the constructive campaign that runs alongside non-violent agitation and provide both a feeding belt of activists and a sense of achievement when political action meets probably unavoidable reverses. It is a policy that embraces the whole of society – including women, children, the old and disabled.

In non-violent actions, training of at least a core group is central – it was mostly in areas where there were no trained activists that violence broke out in India. At the same time, acting openly allows mass involvement through open communication to participants, and allows actions to assume a certain ritualistic nature because there is no hidden intention against the opponent. This allows for flexibility, prevents authoritarianism within the movement and ill-feeling with the opponent, thus allowing for compromise. The nature of these actions is to have limited objectives, as was the case in the Salt March, for example, yet the symbolic power of these actions is not to be underestimated.

Another key idea is the attitude of mind. Much is said about humiliation in situations of occupation, and it certainly happens. However, of Gandhi's terms in prison, Ronald Duncan wrote, 'he spoke of his prison days with joy and with genuine gratitude to those who had detained him. You cannot punish a man who is grateful for his punishment and insists on regarding his jailer as his host. Every privation only enriched him. His dignity lay in his acceptance of every humiliation.'

Finally, the fundamental psychological change that is needed is to see the opponent in a different light. In the context of Palestine, I find it hard to see non-violence as being a central movement while Palestinians (and Israelis) see the Other as being disconfirming and needing to be removed. The British had somewhere to leave to. The Israelis, whatever people may say about 'Going back to Europe', are here and are not likely to be driven into the sea. Such rhetoric hardens attitudes to the current point where Israelis do not particularly care who they upset or kill, because they feel they have no alternative but a future of continued aggression. Gandhi said, 'We want freedom of our country, but not at the expense of the exploitation of the other, and not to degrade other countries. I do not want freedom of India if it means the extinction of England or the disappearance of Englishmen.' Substitute 'Palestine', 'Israel' and 'Israelis' into that and say it a few times.

It is here that I take Gandhi's injunction to convert the opponent literally. It must be clear to anyone of good sense by now that the Children of Israel have been brought back to Palestine to become Muslims. Us calling for their deaths is extremely bad PR. Woody Allen once quipped that he wouldn't want to join any club that would have him as a member. How much less would he, or anyone, want to join a club that wanted to kill him? Seeing the Children of Israel as opponents to be converted, rather than enemies to be killed, would release within us the capacity for change within ourselves, the change of heart, that is so desperately needed to really show the world that Islam is a religion of peace. The non-violent activist 'aiming to convert their opponent, must always themselves remain open to conversion.'

This, I believe, is what is meant by the Third Way and I think it would work. As Gandhi said, 'The right action contains its own propaganda and needs no other.'

And, insha'Allah, I think it's the right time, too.

POWER

It is very hot in the jeep, but at least they are leaving. And there have been no incidents. They didn't find the man they wanted. There was no shooting at them. Not even any stones. Nothing. Boring. Good!

One of the soldiers looks ahead through the front windscreen, scouring the roadside for signs of danger. A rubbish container has been overturned and bags and rubbish are scattered across the road. Like that's going to stop us!

The jeep drives straight through them.

Bang! Then there's a loud hiss. The soldiers jump, expecting a roadside bomb, or a gas canister. But the hiss is a tire going down. In fact, it's two.

We've got two tires out, shouts the driver.

The rubbish bags. They're full of spikes.

The jeep is crippled. The radio operator calls for help. ASAP. So that means half an hour.

The soldiers are waiting. If it's an ambush, and it probably is, shooting will start any moment. Or they'll be the crashing of rocks on the jeep's sides and roof. Not dangerous, but loud. Yeah, and scary. Soldiers check safety catches. Some sip warm, plastic water from their canteens. Nothing happens.

Suddenly a bottle comes in an arc through the air towards them. Petrol bomb. It's a good shot. It lands on the jeep's bonnet. The driver braces himself for a fireball, but the bottle sits there. Beads of sweat trickle off the soldiers' foreheads. And they trickle off the bottle's sides. There's a note in Hebrew on it. It says, Cold water. In case you're thirsty.

It's a trap. You don't get out because they can shoot you then. The bottle sits there mocking you.

There's a movement to the right behind a pile of rubble. Where's our back up? We've got to get out of here before it gets nasty.

Suddenly a sign is raised from behind the rubble.

Would you like your tires mended? It says in immaculate Hebrew.

The sign goes down. Another comes up.

Really! No charge.

Odd. These people are... organised. Before the soldiers can do anything, three figures break cover, one carrying something that looks like a submachine gun, and the others carrying something big. It's a spare wheel. Oh, and it's not a gun. It's a car jack, and he's got a spanner in the other hand. They jog up to the jeep and the expression on their faces can only be described as ... enthusiasm. For the soldiers who have a few words of Arabic, in the context of the Liberation of Palestine, those two concepts together – organisation[13] and enthusiasm[14] - are quite scary.

Ten minutes later, the jeep drives off with its new tires. Children line the road waving and carrying banners saying, Don't come back. Then the road sweepers come out, separating the rubbish for recycling, picking out the crushed metal spikes for mending, and the intact ones for reuse.

And then I wake up. There's shooting outside.

[13] Think, Palestine Liberation Organisation
[14] In Arabic, *Hamas*

THE SIGN OF THREE

She stops wiping the table and cocks her head to one side. So, you're a storyteller, she says. Perhaps you'd like to hear a story?

My new house servant. Now she's a storyteller. OK, I say, even though I'm on my way out.

Let's say there's this guy, she starts. It doesn't have to be a guy, but let's say there's this guy…

She's rather confident, this woman. Considering it's her first time out of Kwazulu.

…There's this guy and he turns up at the gate of this landowner. Looks like he's come a long way. Not from round here. The landowner comes down to the gate with two workers. All armed. The guy at the gate is on his own.

I picture the guy-at-the-gate. Shortish. Checked shirt. Moustache. Not very prepossessing.

She continues, The guy at the gate doesn't speak, but points to three small holes drilled in the upright of the gate, and another one underneath.

She looks at me again, cocks her head again and asks me, What do you think that means?

I've no idea, I reply.

It's a Christian thing. In the Zionist Church anyway. (Ironic, given where we are, I'm thinking). Three running into one.

Running?

Yeah, like blood, she continues. The guy pulls out a small knife and shows it to the landowner. Then he speaks for the first time. Just three words: You stole land, he says. In the blade of the knife there are three holes and one underneath. He mimes a stabbing motion at the man's neck, and bulges his eyes.

Get out of here, the landowner says.

The boss guy and his workers walk back up the road of the settlement with their guns. But they're the ones who are worried.

That's the story.

I don't get it, I say. There must be more to it than that. It's not a full story.

Listen, she says. The guys both come from the same place, right? The one with land knows he's done something wrong and now it looks like it's caught up with him. He understands that from what little the guy at the gate says and does. It's psychological. And there's this juju power, you know, that African thing. Maybe that's enough to freak the guy. And then maybe the guy at the gate *can* get to him. I mean, he'd got that far, and he'd put holes in the gate. And maybe he dreamt it. I don't know. It's a story, man. You don't get everything explained in stories. You have to use your head.

So who is this land-stealing guy?

He was from South Africa. Your country, she says, cocking her head again, so that the pendant around her neck swings visible. It's a small knife blade, with a three-hole, one-hole pattern drilled in it.

That's all I know, she continues.

Then she smiles and says, Perhaps it's you!

III. POETIC PLAYOUT

HIS STORY[15]

They interrupt me
Their car at the checkpoint at one in the morning
Annoys me straight off
So I can't be doing
With agitation
And I'm yawning
And I ask, Where are you going?
I speak in Hebrew because I don't know Arabic
And they are crying and trying
To get me to hurry.
To the hospital, they say
But I'm not doing with that
I'm in charge here and I'll have you remember that
I'm the last line of defence
But I always try to look relaxed
And they're screaming and pointing to the back
Before the IDs, please…
Our baby's ill
We need to get there
Before it's too late
I say, Give me the IDs
And I make them wait
And search the trunk
And they're getting desperate
And I'm watching him
And I tell him to stop yelling
He could do anything
And so I don't do anything
Quickly
But it's her who grabs me
And points to the baby
So I point my gun at her
And she backs away
And I look at the baby anyway and he doesn't look too good
So I say, I'll get the IDs
And have one last look

---

[15] *Based on 'It's from Allah, the soldier said' by Gideon Levy, Ha'aretz, Apr 6 2007*

Under the spare wheel
And then the child is suddenly still.

They check for his pulse
But it's gone
And she cries and says, Our baby is dead!
And he says to her, Be patient, be strong
It's ok it's ok, we're on our way
And ok, so this time it's not a trick
And I say, Get to the hospital quick
And I go to have a cigarette.

He looks like stone
And she cries
When they come back through two hours later
I ask, What happened to the baby?
He says, Our baby died
And I ask why
He looks at me and says
Because you made us wait here 20 minutes
And I say,
It wasn't me
It was from Allah.
I don't speak the language
But as you can see
I'm getting the culture.

THE ANATOMY OF LONGING

I am going to be like a scientist
(She can cry
Not I)
We will take some numbers
This one tells us much
See how big it is
Compared to this one
Longer, rounder
(Do I smell food?)

Enough
Let us move one step away
And talk of names
The naming of parts
Of who we are
And where
(No, the oudh does not sound like a guitar)
We are from

And let us look at the term
That suffered collateral damage
No, it is a joke!
No-one died!
(Of course, they did
That's why they left
My grandmother for one)
From that book
(The curtain flaps in the breeze
Just like the one in my old room)

So, to conclude
What is in a name?
Nothing
It is dead
I have cut out the letters
Like bones
And now the soul is gone
It probably died in that place

Unfortunately, I do not belong
It is an interesting case
And what is that water on my face?

GOD IS NOT AN ELEPHANT (BUT HE IS IN THE ROOM)

At the inter-faith conference
All hell was breaking loose
As men of faith failed to convince each other
Of which was God's preferred people
Or favourite Prophet
Or most desired form of worship
So,
One stood up and said,
I will tell you a story
And because they all liked stories
They shut up and let him speak and he said:
There were some men of faith in a room
And there was an elephant there but it was dark
So they could not see it
But they knew something was there
So they all said:
Describe it!

The Orthodox Christian said:
It is like a piece of rope,
To which the Catholic said:
No, not like rope but a snake.
Indeed not, said the Protestant,
Long and straight maybe
But not a snake or a rope but smooth
And it jabs my finger sharply;
It is like a sword.
The Orthodox Jew said:
No, it is not like that at all.
It is like a wall,
While the liberal Jew said:
Not so! 'Tis like a ball!
The Sunni Muslim said:
If you could see
you'd know like me
that it is like a tree.
The other Muslim said:
What nonsense!

It is like parchment!
He was Shia
And was, of course, holding the ear,
The Sunni, the leg,
The Jews, the side and the head,
And the Christians, respectively,
The tail, the trunk and tusk which,
If nothing else,
At least all began with ‘t’.

Like you perhaps
They recognised the tale –
The Jews, thinking of jokes about
Two Jews,
Three opinions
And four Prime Ministers,
Said:
It is a Jewish story
(Perhaps not actually but metaphorically)
The Christians could not agree naturally and said:
It is **our** story
And describes our curious trinity.
And a Muslim shouted out:
Actually, it is **our** story!
It is Sufi!
Which was met by a loud retort from another brother of that faith
(Wahabi, probably)
That that meant the story was wrong absolutely
As it had not been recorded by Muslim or Bukhari

And so what happened to these men
Was that the conference ended there and then
Not only could they not agree
They could not even let the story be
And so went home
Quite angrily
(There but for the grace of God go we)

THE FAST SHOW (RAMADHAN 2005)

To be read in Northern accent a la Paul Whitehouse

In the land of Jesse's diet
This month I have mostly been eating
Nothing
All Prophets to go to Jerusalem
Which is nice
In fact it's brilliant!

This country is only the size of Wales
And there's so much to think and see
So many things are the size of Wales
Like the amount of Amazon burnt each day
Or Belgium
But it's not like that here – not enough trees
(Bloke strides past flashing landscape images)
But you can still be in the mountains one day
And next in the lowest point of the world
And there's a sea
You can't sink in
And an oasis and
A castle on top of a mountain
Where everyone killed themselves!
Fantastic!

And in the street there's lots of bangs, right,
And you never know what they are
It might be a bloke shooting his Uzi out of a car
For a wedding, right,
On the wedding night
Or boys with fireworks
Which they put in bottles, right
Like, every night
Or it might be a firefight…
And they announced the deaths from the mosque when it got light.

There's places here that are really famous

Even for people who don't believe
Like Nazareth and Bethlehem and Jerusalem and you can go to them
'Go right down to the middle of the West Bank
That's where you have to catch a tank'
To Tel Aviv
Fantastic!
And last week there was a t-shirt in my head that said
'Too much Tel aviV is bad for your eyes'
And that's copyright
And you ain't seen it, right!
And Duran Duran did a song called 'Tel Aviv',
Which is about right.
(In fact, it was all right.)

And I can't sleep much at night
I lie down and my head is telling me
Write it down
Write down that Egypt in the Bible represents
The unintegrated unconscious aspect of the persona
Of a people who've always been in tents
And about how the writers of the Bible
Condemned coming generations
To years of analysis and morbid introspection
And about how Freud thought even Moses was Egyptian
And this is at 4.30 in the morning for God's Sake
And that's why I came here and it suits me (mostly)
And it's brilliant
And that was yesterday
And today I'm sitting here writing again
My first poem in ten years
And it's brilliant
(Writing, anyway,
Not the poem, necessarily)
And I've got this plan
(Bloke still striding past flashing landscape images)
Of buying a bike and cycling to the north of the country
And then cycling down
Past the Galilee and Jericho and the Dead Sea
Because in 1981
Just before uni

I walked all that way
With an American Jew
And I didn't even know that
Or what that meant
And I didn't know that
It wasn't exactly one country
Or even two but, in a way, three
(Look at the map and you'll see)
But we walked it anyway
And we'd walk and we'd look over Jordan and we'd see
Not a band of angels coming out for me, no,
We saw
Jordan
The country
And we'd say, Wow, that's, like,
Jordan.
Fantastic.
Because we were kibbutz volunteers
And it hadn't occurred to us that
Actually we were not just everywhere
But somewhere
And we walked over 300 miles to prove it
and we didn't have enough to talk about
So we tried to learn
German
And other languages
And in the desert it was scorchio
And I didn't drink enough
And the sun shone and it was brilliant in the hot way
And I had lots of injections in the place
The sun don't shine
And it wasn't brilliant it was rubbish
And at the end we jogged the last 10 ks
And near the end said,
Brilliant, we can do anything, and at the end
We couldn't even find the energy to collapse
And that's why I think
It's the most interesting country in the world
And why on earth I'm here
And the sun still shines and

It’s brilliant
And there’s a danger
That I might not be able to think everything
And get it all sorted out in my head
Or on paper
Because everything happens so fast inside you here
When you fast
And at all the other times as well
And perhaps like many others here
I will go a little mad
And forget how to spell
And think in automatic.
And become a fanatic!
Fantastic!!

POEM IN THE SKY (@10972 METRES)

flat sea fog island in rolling boil to
massive bank of nuclear mushroom pillars shading
bays and bubbling cotton wool candy floss snow
stark, light-framed toppling plumes poised
to fall into chasm and then flattened misty sea
and on

fluffy buffalo clamber
out of mist and skirt the edge of sea
with massive mothers-a-leaping and merging
to a rush to who knows where
concealed in grey

and a
sudden tower erupts
but is washed under by
unlikely cataract cloudfall rehearsing
a later moment as
rain

four frozen polar bears
race to the ice shelf watching
still distant archipelagos
rings, real ridged rings topped by
frozen explosions of crisply
defined moments

and sudden whiter outgrowths reach up
almost close enough to touch and the mind
will not stop comparing and decoding each and
every unique cloud play up here
and each and every unique cloud play here

it just is and
i will not let it be and
it just is and ever will be
when we've passed
but different

APPENDIX

Thirty-one Years of Journeys to the Holy Land

- October 1981-June 1982: Volunteer on Kibbutz Amiad, Galilee and three weeks in Egypt. Walked the length of Israel, including through the West Bank. (June 1982: Israeli Invasion of Lebanon)

- August 1982: Two weeks on Kibbutz Amiad, after travelling through Eastern Europe, Turkey, Syria and Jordan

- July - December 1985: Two months teaching in Gaza, three months in Jericho and several visits to Amiad

- July - August 1987: International Summer Camp for Volunteers, Bir Zeit University, near Ramallah

- December 1988: One week in Gaza and Jerusalem (1st Anniversary of first Intifada)

- July - September 1993: Gaza Strip, English teaching (Peace Accords signed, Intifada ends)

- September 1993: One week in Sinai

- October – December 1993: Volunteer on Newe Shalom/Wahat a-Salaam, near Jerusalem

- July 1994: One month. Course on Newe Shalom/Wahat a-Salaam in ‘Peacemaking for Community Leaders’. Travelled to Nablus and Gaza.

- April/May 1995: Ten days. Married in Ramallah.

- July/August 1996: Six weeks in Nablus

- July/August 1997: Six weeks in Nablus, teaching English in Jenin

- July/August 1998: Six weeks in Nablus

- August 1999 – July 2000: Teaching English at Bir Zeit University and British Council in Ramallah (September, second Intifada begins)

- April 2003: Three weeks in Nablus

- July/August 2004: Four weeks in Nablus

- September 2005 – July 2007: Two years teaching English in Nablus

- August 2008: Four weeks in Ramallah

- August 2009: Four weeks in Nablus

- October 2009: Sponsored cycle ride from Cairo to Jerusalem

- April 2012: Two weeks in the West Bank

Lightning Source UK Ltd.
Milton Keynes UK
UKOW041104091212

203360UK00001B/26/P

9 781781 767436